Archie and Mary Tisdall have had a life of travel which many would envy. Archie served in the Royal Air Force for forty years and during that time they lived in such diverse countries as Singapore, Jordan, Libya, Tunisia and Malta. Towards retirement they bought a motorcaravan which enabled them to visit further places abroad, principally in Western Europe, and gradually they began to write of their experiences for magazines.

They have travelled extensively in Spain, spending many winters in the Canary Islands. This resulted in 1984 in the publication of two guide books, *Tenerife and the Western Canary Islands:* and *Gran Canaria and the Eastern Canary Islands.* These books are now in their second and third impression. Their love of Spain has also taken them to the Balearic Islands, about which they have written a further three guide books: *Majorca, Menorca* and *Ibiza and Formentera.* The island series continues in their sixth book, *Madeira,* which describes that beautiful Portuguese island and its tiny neighbour Porto Santo.

With this their seventh travel guide, they write about that popular region of mainland Portugal, the Algarve, which they first visited in 1970 and have returned to many times since.

Archie and Mary Tisdall have two sons, two daughters and five grandchildren, and, when not travelling, they live in Salisbury, Wiltshire.

Acknowledgements

The authors would like to thank the following people and organisations for their help, directly or indirectly, in the preparation of this book:

Senhor João Custadio, Director (and Pilar Pereira), The Portuguese National Tourist Office, London; The Director (and Luisa Correia), Região de Turismo do Algarve; The Managers, Thomson Holiday Hotels, Algarve: Thomson Holidays Ltd (Gloria Ward), London. Brittany Ferries, Plymouth.

Our thanks go to our helpful editors, Yvonne Messenger and Bryn Thomas, and to our publisher, Roger Lascelles. Finally we acknowledge the interest and encouragement from our friends and family.

Front cover: *The beautiful country church of São Lourenço, seen from the garden of the Centro Culteral, near Almancil.*

The Algarve

A Travel Guide

Mary and Archie Tisdall

Roger Lascelles, Cartographic and Travel Publisher
47 York Road, Brentford, Middlesex TW8 0QP. Tel: 081-847 0935

Publication Data

Title	The Algarve
Typeface	Phototypeset in Compugraphic Times
Photographs	By the Authors
Index	Jane Thomas
Printing	Kelso Graphics, Kelso, Scotland.
ISBN	0 903909 84 7
Edition	First Sept 90
Publisher	Roger Lascelles
	47 York Road, Brentford, Middlesex, TW8 0QP.
Copyright	Mary & Archie Tisdall

Distribution

Africa:	South Africa —	Faradawn, Box 17161, Hillbrow 2038
Americas:	Canada —	International Travel Maps & Books, P.O. Box 2290, Vancouver BC V6B 3W5
Asia:	India —	English Book Store, 17-L Connaught Circus/P.O. Box 328, New Delhi 110 001
	Singapore —	Graham Brash Pte Ltd., 36-C Prinsep St
Australasia:	Australia —	Rex Publications, 413 Pacific Highway, Artarmon NSW 2064. 428 3566
Europe:	Belgium —	Brussels - Peuples et Continents
	Germany —	Available through major booksellers with good foreign travel sections
	GB/Ireland —	Available through all booksellers with good foreign travel sections
	Italy —	Libreria dell'Automobile, Milano
	Netherlands —	Nilsson & Lamm BV, Weesp
	Denmark —	Copenhagen - Arnold Busck, G.E.C. Gad, Boghallen, G.E.C. Gad
	Finland —	Helsinki — Akateeminen Kirjakauppa
	Norway —	Oslo - Arne Gimnes/J.G. Tanum
	Sweden —	Stockholm/Esselte, Akademi Bokhandel, Fritzes, Hedengrens Gothenburg/Gumperts, Esselte Lund/Gleerupska
	Switzerland —	Basel/Bider: Berne/Atlas; Geneve/Artou; Lausanne/Artou: Zurich/Travel Bookshop

Contents

Contents

Appendices

Index

Foreword

The purpose of this guide book is to enable visitors to get to know the Algarve, how to get there, when to go and, on arrival, what to expect. Much is written here to help tourists have a pleasant holiday. The various types of accommodation are explained and current prices are quoted, though it must be understood that these are always increasing. Shopping areas, markets, souvenirs and good buys are suggested. The cost of car rental, taxis and coach excursions are detailed as well as many sports and entertainments in the resorts.

For those travellers who wish to know more about the Algarve than they can get from holiday brochures, this guide describes day drives and suggested places for walking. Anyone interested in museums, history, flora and fauna of this region will find these subjects covered. A whole chapter gives locations and descriptions of the many camping parks.

Places of interest and the best beaches are listed. An index is helpful in locating subjects and towns.

The average currency exchange rate at the time of writing is £1 : 250 escudos. Facts and information are as accurate as possible in this ever-changing world.

ONE

Introducing the Algarve

The Algarve has much to offer its visitors for it is a gentle land, blessed with a high rate of sunshine and a useful amount of rain. Together these create landscapes of low mountains, thick fragrant forests, attractive farmland with colourful citrus fruit orchards and hedgerows filled with wild flowers. Scattered along the coast and inland are fine old castles, churches and buildings of historic and artistic interest. Museums, art galleries, even Roman ruins, are all here to be enjoyed.

A main attraction is the wonderful coastline offering miles and miles of perfectly clean golden sandy beaches, with inviting little coves and red rock cliffs. For most of the year, the sea is calm, ideal for swimming and watersports, with beaches for soaking up the sun. There are plenty of safe sands for children.

Hotels, apartments and villas provide a range of accommodation. Holidays can be booked in five-star luxury hotels, family and young-at heart hotels, less expensive but clean and pleasant hotels, and in small pensions for those on low budgets. Visitors who prefer self-catering can choose from a huge selection of apartments and villas, most near the tourist resorts, though some have quieter locations. Huge modern tourist complexes, even complete purpose built villages, containing hotels, apartments, shops, restaurants and watersport centres, have been designed for the enjoyment of holidaymakers. The Algarve is a splendid place for camping holidays and whether you are a backpacker, caravanner or motorcaravanner the choice of camping grounds extends right along the coastline.

The restaurants, cafés and bars stay open long hours. Entertainments range from music by a gentle guitarist to casinos and swinging discos.

You'll find an infinite variety of sports, including the latest large water parks. Golfers are in their element with six championship

Steps lead down to this idyllic sandy beach at Praia Santa Ana near Lagos.

courses to choose from, and there are hotels specially designed for professional and amateur golfers and their families.

Inland there is a different Algarve, with quiet villages where streets are cobbled and old ladies dressed in black wear felt hats against the sun's rays. Here you may see an elderly man sitting by the road side, patiently weaving baskets from locally grown cane, oblivious to passers-by. Each day, fresh fish is sold from a travelling van, and at any small restaurant you can enjoy *caldeirada de peixe,* a rich and filling fish stew, or grilled sardines, the staple diet of the Algarvian peasant *(velhote).*

In the highlands, market towns throng with the fresh products of the land: baskets of oranges, apples, peaches and apricots, green beans, spinach and lettuce. There are handicrafts too: hand-carved wooden utensils, copper, brass and bronze ornaments, and hand-painted glazed tiles. You will discover that the local sweet nougat is delicious. The mountain air is fragrant with pine and in early spring the blossom of the almond trees paints the countryside with its delicate pink and white petals.

Some things are so characteristic of the Algarve: graceful filigreed chimneys — never, it seems, are two alike; imposing ochre-coloured medieval churches and castles; fishermen's tiny cottages painted in different pastel shades, with nets hanging out to dry; weird red rock formations, with swirling seas entering deep caverns. These are only some of the things which will make up your memories of the Algarve.

Situation

The Algarve (5,108 sq. km.) is situated in the south of Portugal, which is the most western country in Europe. It stretches from Vila Real de Santo António in the east to Cape São Vicente in the west, a distance of 160km. The maximum distance from the Ribeira do Vascão creek, bordering Alentjo in the north, to Faro in the south is 40km. The northern border is with the province of Lower Alentejo, while to the east is the Rio Guadiana, the border with Spain. With its south and west coast facing the Atlantic Ocean, the Algarve has coastline of 200km which is a pleasant mixture of Mediterranean type golden beaches and wild Atlantic landscapes. The flat eastern area along the coast is called the Sotavento, while west of Faro are sandy coves and cliffs of the Barlavento sector.

Cut off from the rest of Portugal by the Caldeirão and Monchique mountains the Algarve has always had an isolated position. Now with new and faster roads and better communications the Algarve, while retaining its own character, is gradually becoming more part of the European community.

Climatic chart

LAGOS	\multicolumn{4}{c}{Air temperature, average}
	min		max	
	°F	°C	°F	°C
Jan	46.0	7.8	59.3	15.2
Feb	47.3	8.5	61.5	16.4
March	50.7	10.4	64.0	17.8
April	53.9	12.2	68.0	20.0
May	55.7	13.2	70.5	21.4
June	62.0	16.7	78.6	25.9
July	64.2	17.9	82.4	28.0
August	64.7	18.2	83.3	28.5
Sept	62.9	17.2	78.8	26.0
Oct	58.6	14.8	72.8	22.7
Nov	53.0	11.7	66.5	19.2
Dec	48.2	9.0	61.7	16.5

By courtesy of Instituto Nacional de Meteorologia e Geofísica

Climate

The Province of the Algarve has the warmest climate in all Portugal. Despite the fact that it faces the Atlantic Ocean, its climate has the character of the Mediterranean, with temperate winters and long summers that are dry and hot. During the hottest part of the summer, July and August, Atlantic breezes make it pleasant; however, those who are fair-skinned should be careful of sunburn.

The clear air and cloudless skies, together with low humidity, allow the sun's rays to be fierce.

Most rain falls in winter, particularly in the *serra* or mountain region of Monchique and Caldeirão. These mountains protect the beaches from the most common wind that comes from the north. In winter the sea temperature, affected by the Gulf Stream, rarely drops below 50°F (15°C). The Levante is a chilly and damp wind which in winter can bring heavy rains; but in summer the Levante may contain a fine dry sand from the Sahara. Generally temperature in the four winter months rarely goes below 54°F (12°C). In summer it can rise to 84°F (28°C).

A glance at the Algarve

This summary of interesting places to visit aims to give you a quick introduction to the Algarve. All the places mentioned here are described more fully in later chapters (see index). Distances given are from the provincial capital, Faro.

Faro The capital of the Algarve is surprisingly quiet for such an important place. Many fine old buildings including the cathedral, museums, Tourist Information Office and a pedestrian shopping precinct. Airport 7km. Nearby Ilha de Faro, a holiday beach resort on a spit of land reached by a causeway, has camping.

Eastern Algarve
Alcoutim 92km: On the north eastern border with Spain (San Lucar de Guadiana). This very fine old village dating back to Roman times has, as its position expects, an old castle and ancient church. Here you see almond trees and grazing sheep.
Castro Marim 61km: This town 10km north of Vila Real de Santo António, on the N122, was once important to the Romans and Moors. King João IV and King Alfonso III both built castles here, and there are substantial remains. The town has narrow streets and good views of the Rio Guadiana and nearby Guadiana Nature Reserve.
Estoi 11km: Inland from Faro. Visit the sadly neglected but fascinating eighteenth-century Palace of Estoi, a wonderful example of different styles of both architecture and garden ornaments.

Milreu 10km: On the western outskirts of Estoi. The Roman ruins of Milreu will interest historians. You can see the sunken bath and temple.

Monte Gordo 45km: On the EN125 it's the largest tourist development east of Faro. Wide sandy beach, hotels, casino and camping.

Olhão 9km: A distinctive fishing port with strong North African style of flat cube dwellings, large markets, busy streets and little tourist development.

São Bras de Alportel 16km: In attractive countryside to the north of Faro, this quiet town is surrounded by orange and almond groves. The Pousada (government hotel) sits on a hill to the north, with extensive views from the gardens.

Tavira 28km: Possibly the most interesting town in the Algarve. The Rio Gilao divides this town which has many fine seventeenth- and eighteenth-century churches. Attractive and ancient houses with different types of roofs. Tourist Information Office.

Vila Real de Santo António 51km: The border town where you can take a ferry across the Rio Guadiana to Ayamonte in Spain. Eighteenth-century buildings and a fine central square. Busy with shoppers from Spain. Tourist Information Office.

Central Algarve

Albufeira 35km: The Algarve's premier tourist attraction, once a tiny fishing port and still pleasant except on the outskirts where mass development has swallowed the countryside. Good for beach, shopping, market, hotels, apartments, restaurants, discos, nightlife, amusements and camping. Tourist Information Office.

Armação de Pera 45km: Pleasant fishing village and seaside resort with long golden sands. Many highrise hotels, apartments, restaurants and bars. Camping.

Almancil 13km: West of Faro, on the busy EN125. Noted for its São Lourenço Church, to the east of town, a tiny beautiful Baroque gem of blue glazed tiles and gilt carved altar. Down the lane visit Centro Cultural Centre and Arts Centre.

Carvoeiro 77km: Small fishing village and beach, now developed with attractive villas, apartments and tourist clubs.

Loulé 17km: Old inland town with restored castle. Narrow streets where artisans still work. Moorish style market. Festival of Flowers in February. Sixteenth-century church.

Quarteira 20km: Seaside resort with long promenade, fishing boats and fish market in old quarter. Camping on hill in pine woods.

Quinta do Largo 15km: Large tourist complex, luxury hotels, apartments, villas, golf, riding, tennis. Set in 2,000 acres of pine hills. Playground of the rich and famous.

Silves 55km: No visitor to the Algarve should miss this fine inland city founded by the Phoenicians. The restored castle and thirteenth-century cathedral are set on a hill above the main shopping area. Busy market by river front. Tourist Information Office.

Vale do Lobo 25km: Valley of the Wolf, where expensive hotels, apartments and villas cater for rich tourists. Excellent sports facilities.

Vilamoura 30km: One of Europe's most modern and largest developments. This 4,000-acre enterprise contains watersport centre, yacht marina, luxury hotels, apartments, small shops and golf courses.

Western Algarve

Aljezur 110km: This small town on the EN120, site of old copper mines, has a ruined castle and Tourist Information Office. Along the coast there are kilometres of undeveloped beaches and pinewoods. A peaceful, remote and sometimes windy area. Nearby camping.

Alvor 76km: Said to have been founded in 436 AD. It now has a five-star hotel on the low cliffs, a sandy beach and good views of the Monchique mountains. Cobble streets in the old town.

Barrangem do Arade 65km: This large reservoir and pinewoods between Silves and Alte makes a pleasant picnic place. Restaurant and good views.

Cabo de São Vicente 120km: The most westerly point of the Algarve, with its fortress and lighthouse, lonely, wild and often windy. The pounding seas and high cliffs make a thrilling spectacle.

Caldas de Monchique 83km: It is a lovely country drive to this famous, ancient mountain spa. The water is still bottled here. Nearby the town of Monchique is a centre of handicrafts and seventeenth-century architecture.

Fóia 87km: An obelisk marks this highest spot in the Algarve (902m). From the rock viewpoint there is a panorama of the coastline.

Lagoa 55km: This town, on the EN125, is best known for the co-operative wine cellars Adegas: it is also an important market centre.

Lagos 78km: One of the nicest places in the Algarve, the town lies by the Rio Bensafrim. Historic links, colourful market, narrow cobble streets, pedestrian shopping centre, interesting churches, museums, Tourist Information Office and camping.

Portimão 76km: At the mouth of Rio Arade. A busy fish seaport, with difficult parking. Good place for shopping, restaurants and Tourist Information Office.

Praia da Luz 87km: Attractive white village, family tourist resort with good sandy beach.

Praia da Rocha 88km: Major family tourist resort. Immense sandy beach with low red and yellow cliffs and attractive rock formations. Hotels, restaurants and bars.

Sagres 114km: Well known as place where Prince Henry established his School of Navigation. Visit the seventeenth-century fortress. Busy fishing port; swordfish and lobsters at the fish market.

Set in a prominent position, close to the Cathedral in the Largo da Sé, Faro, is this fine statue of Francisco Gomes, 1739-1816.

Beaches

There are flags on beaches to signal whether bathing is safe or not.
- **Red** — This is the **danger** flag. Bathing is forbidden.
- **Yellow** — There is some danger so **take care.** Swimming is forbidden but you may paddle.
- **Green** — It is **safe.** Swimming is allowed.
- **Blue and white** — This chequered flag means that the life guard is absent.

The following list describes beaches of the Algarve from east to west. Beaches have been given the following symbols:

S = Beach is signposted	F = Flags in season
B = Beach bar	E = Windsurfing
R = Restaurant	G = Lifeguard in season

Manta Rota: Off the E125. Entrances are also marked Cacela, Velha, Alagoa, Praia Verde, Guincho and Monte Gordo. Ten kilometres of sand and dunes. Surf. Manta Rota is a good beach for children. S.B.R.F.E.G.

Cabanas: Across the estuary. Clean beach with sand dunes. S.B.R.F.

Pedras d'el Rey: Off the EN125, through the complex and a fair walk. Good wind surfing, (wind in afternoon). S.B.E.

Fuseta: Off the EN125, the beach is on the lagoon, with good windsurfing. S.E.

Praia de Faro: Long stretch of sand, south of Faro, across the causeway. S.B.R.

Quinta do Largo: Approach from Almancil. Pine trees, sea water lakes, good surf. S.B.R.E.

Duras Dourados: Approach from Almancil and turn off before Vale do Lobo. B.

Vale do Lobo: Approach from Almancil. Long sandy beach, dunes and cliffs. generally good surfing. S.B.R.F.E.G.

Quarteira: The beach adjoins the town. Fishing port. Dunes and low cliffs. Calm and excellent for children. S.B.R.F.G.E.

Praia da Marinha (Vilamoura): Beyond Casino and in front of Hotel Atlantis and Dom Pedro. Quiet with breakwaters. Very suitable for infants. S.B.R.F.E.G.

Vilamoura (Falésia): In Vilamoura. beach with dunes, windy. Surfing. Nice for children. Car park. S.B.R.F.E.G.

Aldeia das Açoleias (Falésia): Between Vilamoura and Albufeira. Park at top of beach. Cliffs behind clean sand. Surfing. Suitable for children. S.B.F.E.G.

Olhos de Água: Off the Vilamoura to Albufeira road. Good parking. Fishing port. Poor swimming. To the east is the long beach of Falésia. S.B.R.

Praia da Balaia: At the Bullring, Montechoro, turn towards Olhos d'Agua. The beach is through the hotel complex. Good walks. S.B.R.F.E.G.

Praia da Oura: Below Montechoro Hotel and 3km east of Albufeira. Car park, clean, suitable for children and busy. S.B.R.F.E.G.

Albufeira: Through the tunnel under the cliffs from the town. Sand. Busy, no parking. R.F.E.G.

Praia da Baleeira: Towards Pêra from Albufeira. Diving in clear and calm sea.

Praia do Rafeal: On the road to Pêra, 3km from Albufeira. Sheltered and suitable for children. Boat launch. S.B.R.

Praia do Castelo: Turn off for Galé and left past Quinta da Gale and Torre. Small and sheltered. Walks and climbs. B.R.

Praia da Galé: Access 2km from the Albufeira to Pêra road at Vale de Parro. Rocks S.B.R.

Plenty of space for everyone on the clean, soft sands and only a short walk to the hotel, at Monte Gordo.

Armação de Pêra: Three kilometres from EN125. Car park, fishing fleet and market. No rocks. Surf, fishing. Fine for children. S.B.R.F.E.G.

Senhora da Rocha, Cova Redonda and Tremossos: From Porches on EN125, take the Armação de Pêra road. At Hotel Viking follow Praia da Rocha sign. Caves and swimming. S.B.R.F.G.

Praia de Albufeira, Baraquinho Fontainhas: Coves, caves and cliff walks. B.R.

Marinha: Between Porches and Lagoa. Before Benagil turn left and park on cliff top. Walk down to beaches. Suitable for children. R.

Benagil: From Lagoa road, turn off 2km before Carvoeiro. Fishing fleet. B.

Carvalho: Near Alfanzina. You walk from the road to Benagil. A tunnel leads to a little smugglers beach. B.R.

Centianes: About 4km east of Carvoeiro. Small, sandy with good surf. S.B.R.

Carvoeiro: At Lagoa turn off the EN125. Small car park, sand and fishing boats. B.R.F.G.

Ferragudo (Praia Grande): At Portimão Bridge continue for 5km past village. Car park. Sandy, fine for children. S.B.R.E.

Praia da Rocha: Take the main beach road from Portimão. Parking and steps down to probably the most popular and sometimes crowded beach. Surf and children's amusements. B.R.F.E.G.

Praia do Vau (João de Aréns): West of Praia da Rocha. Small coves with clifftop views. Suitable for children. B.R.F.G.

Praia de Alvor, Três Irmãos: Reached along cliff road west of Praia da Rocha or through Alvor village. Sand and safe surfing. S.B.R.F.E.G.

Praia Meia and S. Roque: East from Lagos. Car park. One of the longest beaches. Dunes and surfing. Currents can be dangerous for children.

Praia da Batata, Pinhão: West of Lagos at top of hill. Park off road, walk down to sandy coves and quiet surf. Suitable for children. B.R.F.G.

Dona Ana: To the west of Lagos, from Sagres exit, signposted Praia d'Ana, Porto de Mos. Car park near Hotel Golfino. Steps down to sandy beach, safe for children. S.B.R.F.G.

Praia da Luz: Turn left at Espiche. Small car park. Fishing boats, quiet surf, suitable for children. S.B.R.F.G.

Burgau: Cliff road from Praia da Luz or left off main road. Restricted parking. Fishing port and sand. Good for children. S.B.R.F.G.

Boca do Rio: Turn left at Budens crossroads, continue for 5km. Rough road. Large carpark. Surfing, suitable for children. B.

Salema: Between Budens and Figueira. Village adjoins beach. Good surf, fishing boats. Suitable for children. S.B.R.F.G.

Figueira: Rough track leads from Figueira bus stop. Walkers only. Rocky and not for children.

Zavial: Near Ingrin. Small car park. Flat, sandy and nice for children. S.B.R.

Ingrinha, Barranco João Vaz: On main road 5km from Raposeira. Limited parking. Pebble coves, no surf, skin-diving and walking, fine for children. S.B.

Martinhal: Two kilometres before Sagres. Car park. Dunes, sheltered by harbour and fine for children. S.B.R.

Baleeira: Below hotel. Small and no surf. B.R.

S Mareta: Turn left at Sagres lighthouse roundabout. Large car park. Sand, safe for children. S.R.B.F.G.

Praia do Tonel: Near Sagres lighthouse. Small car park. Path leads to sandy beach and rocks. Not safe when windy or for children.

Belixe: Five kilometres north of Sagres. Car park. Path down to sandy beach. Surf with no rocks. Can be windy. Good for children. S.B.R.

Offshore beaches

Armona, Culatra and Faro Islands: These three islands are reached by ferry from Olhão during the summer. The ticket office is behind the Galp Petrol Station. Ferries go about every two hours. Sandy beaches with dunes. B.R.

Tavira: The small islands off Tavira have beaches suitable for swimming. They are reached by boat from the town.

The west coast

The western coastline has 40km of Atlantic sandy shore, undeveloped and rarely visited. Those with access along unmade roads are **Arrifana, Monte Clérigo, Amoreira** and **Praia de Odeceixe.**

TWO

Planning your holiday

When to go

When you look at the climatic chart, you will see that it never gets extremely cold in the Algarve, and snow and frost are rare except on the highest peaks. If you like a moderate climate then certainly from January to May will be pleasant. January and February see the almond blossom and March and April are wonderful months for wild flowers: inland the lower slopes are a mass of flowering wild shrubs. Comes May, and with the lengthening days the temperature rises. June, July and September bring really hot sunshine. Then it's October time, when the air is fresh and bright. November can bring rain storms but in between the sun will shine. Winter evenings can be chilly enough for a topcoat and indoor heating.

The main tourist season is from April to the end of October, but increasingly the package holiday firms are offering good bargain holidays in the winter. The Algarve is an all year round venue for campers; all the sites remain open although most have reduced facilities during the winter months.

What to pack

Your choice of clothes will depend on the time of year when you visit the Algarve. From June to September you can count on warm weather every day; you will need a cardigan or jacket only when visiting inland mountain areas. Outside these months you will need to take warmer clothing. The most comfortable clothing for hot weather is cotton or natural fibres; if you use man-made synthetics, the loose styles will feel more comfortable. The same applies to footwear; do not take tight fitting shoes as feet will tend to swell in the warmth. For long walks strong footwear is required.

Seen in many of the older villages is the distinctly Moorish influence of many houses with colour wash walls, flat roof, terrace, the blue and white azulejos tiles and ornate doorways.

Nowadays the wearing of bikinis, even topless, is becoming accepted on the quieter beaches. But when walking in the streets a shirt or cotton top should be worn over swim wear. Churches no longer require women visitors to cover their heads, but modesty and a decorous manner are expected. Evening wear is mostly casual; in the five-star hotels and when visiting casinos men may be required to wear ties and jackets. In the evening if eating outside, some sort of shawl or jacket may be needed.

Remember to take a sunhat and sunglasses (though these can be bought locally). Suntan oils and creams are a necessity, unless you are already very tanned. Some anti-mosquito cream may be useful, too. No need to pack quantities of toothpaste, soap or shampoo for plenty of brands are sold in the Algarve, though prices can be higher.

Even the most amateur of photographers will wish to pack a camera, for the Algarve has potential for marvellous holiday snaps, If you wish for something of better quality, the strong light and sparkling seas will require a light density filter. All popular sizes of films are available, but with prices higher than at home. In the main resorts a twenty-four hour developing service is usual.

You may wish to take some reading matter. English paperbacks, newspapers and magazines can be purchased, though usually at a higher price than in the UK. A Portuguese/English phrase book will be useful if you wish to make contact with the locals, especially when visiting inland Portugal. Travel into the mountains will be enhanced if you take your binoculars.

Pipe smokers will find that Portuguese tobacco is similar to Dutch tobacco; cigarette smokers will probably arrive with duty free smokes bought on the aircraft. There are a number of brands of Portuguese cigarettes to be found in the Algarve.

Budgeting for your holiday

The cost of living should not prove higher in the Algarve than elsewhere in Europe or the UK. Generally speaking, package tour holidaymakers require spending money for entertainments, drinks and possibly additional meals, unless the package includes full board. Eating out in the Algarve need not be expensive. You must include extra costs such as taking part in sports, excursions, the hire of sun umbrellas and chairs, laundry and tips *(gorjetas)* for waiters, taxi drivers and porters (about 10 per cent is sufficient); and maybe for some extra film for the camera and for buying souvenirs and presents to take home.

Prices in tourist areas will be a few escudos higher than in the country or towns like Faro and Lagos, but if one takes into consideration the extra cost of travelling to a non-tourist area to shop it will probably work out about the same. For the independent traveller it is possible to live quite cheaply especially by purchasing local foods, many of which are less expensive than in the UK. Bars and restaurants are less costly and generally give a cheerful and good service.

Tourist information

You do not need a visa to stay in the Algarve for up to sixty days if you hold a British passport. Your passport should be stamped at your point of entry (airport or frontier). This period of sixty days may be extended on application to the Foreigners Registration Service (Serviço de Estrangeiros e Frontieras) before the expiry of the initial period. The office in Faro is at Rua Jose de Matos, 14. Open Monday to Friday 0900 to 1200 and 1400 to 1700 hrs. Tel: 089 27822. There are also offices at Vila Real de Santo António. Tel: 081 4341, Albufeira. Tel: 089 53344 and Portimão. Tel: 082 25400.

Some other European passport holders may need a visa; it is advisable to check with the **Portuguese Consulate General,** 62 Brompton Road, London SW3. Tel: 071-581 8722. This also applies to those intending to work (or take up work) in the Algarve.

If you are staying in a hotel, residential apartments or on a campsite the receptionist will fill in a White Registration Card that includes your arrival and departure dates. It is advisable to see that this is done, especially if you have failed to get your passport stamped on entry. The officials are sometimes lax about doing this.

Vaccinations are not normally needed for the Algarve, only in the case of an epidemic would they be required. Up-to-date tourist information and leaflets can be obtained from the **Portuguese National Tourist Office,** New Bond Street House, 1-5 New Bond Street, London W1Y 0NP (entrance in Burlington Gardens) Tel: 071-493 3873. The office is open Monday to Friday between 0930 and 1730 hrs. It is closed on public holidays and on 10 June, which is the Portuguese National Day.

Duty Free Allowance into the UK

300 cigarettes or 75 cigars or 400 grms of tobacco

5 litres of still wine

1½ litres of spirits over 22% or 3 litres
below 22% (eg fortified or sparkling wine)
or a further 3 litres of wine

Perfume 90 cc

Toilet water 375 cc

Other goods, £250 worth, but no more than 50 litres
of beer, or more than 25 mechanical lighters.

Duty Free Allowance into Portugal

200 cigarettes or 250 grms of tobacco

2 bottles of table wine

1 bottle of spirits

Perfume 50 grams

Toilet water ¼ litre

Note that it is forbidden to take fresh meat into
the Algarve. Small quantities of tea and coffee for
personal use only may be taken in.

Tourist information offices in the Algarve

The main tourist office is in Faro: the **Região de Turismo do
Algarve,** Rua de Misercórdia. Tel: 089 2504 and 24067. It is close
to the centre of Faro and near the seafront and port. Open from
0900 to 1900 hrs Monday to Friday. 0900 to 1200 and 1430 to 1700
hrs on Saturday (closed on public holidays). Other information
offices are in Albufeira, Aljezur, Armação de Pera, Lagos,
Portimâo, Praia da Rocha, Silves, Tavira, Vila Real de Santo
António, Olhão, Quarteira, Carvoeiro, Loulé and the airport.

The Portuguese Tourist Office is an official government
department with English-speaking staff who will give free
information, maps and leaflets. They have lists of hotels and other

accommodation and will make reservations for you to stay in the state owned *pousadas* (country inns). They also have bus and train timetables, routes and information about special events of interest, such as walks, shows, concerts, exhibitions and festivals.

Package holidays

Nearly all the UK companies that operate package holidays include the Algarve. They offer holidays throughout the year and generally provide very good value for money. Caravela, Martyn Holidays and Meon Villas and Apartments are tour operators who specialise in packages to the Algarve.

By booking this type of holiday it allows you to budget in advance for most of your expenses. When you book a package the cost includes accommodation, air fare, airport taxes and transport to and from your destination in the Algarve and airport, which may be either Faro or Lisbon. Tour operators' brochures, obtained from UK travel agents, give details of flights, type of resort, star-rating of hotel or apartment, meal arrangements and what you can expect in the way of entertainment and sport. Because of the many facilities for golf and tennis some hotels cater specially for those who wish to pursue these sports.

On arrival at the airport you will be met by the tour company representative. He or she will assist you to a coach which will take you to your accommodation. This courier will meet you again for a welcoming party when you will be informed of local interests, excursions and entertainments.

It is recommended that you use the services of your courier who has up-to-date information on the locality and about good eating places. These representatives are generally helpful, hard working and patient.

Some of the holiday firms offer two centre package deals, with one week in Lisbon, the capital of Portugal, and another in the Algarve. Thomson Holidays, who claim a large percentage of the market, issue a Young-at-Heart brochure to cater for those who expect entertainment within their hotel.

Travel agents

There are a number of travel agents *(Viagens)* in the resorts along the Algarve. Their services vary. They may be agents for hotels, apartments, flight reservations, self-drive car rental, coach excursions, sea-fishing expeditions and currency exchange. Many of their staff speak English. Offices are open from 0900 to 1230 and from 1430 to 1800 hrs, Monday to Friday and some are open on Saturday morning. Amongst the travel agents are:

Viagens e Turismo Algarve Marina, Centro Comercial, Vilamoura. Tel: 089 32772.

Internacional Viagens Rua Vitor da Costa e Silva 6, Lagos. Tel: 082 62051 and 62650.

Viagens Rawes Rua Conselheiro Bivar 72/78, Faro. Tel: 089 23195

Viagens Rawes Rua da Hortinha 34, Portimão.

Ouratours Areias S. João, Albufeira.

Delta Viagens e Turismo Praça de Touros de Albufeira, Shop 22, Albufeira. Tel. 089 54881.

The new yacht marina at the modern, purpose built holiday complex of Vilamoura, is already proving very popular with various sized vessels.

Taking the children

Children of all ages will really enjoy being in the Algarve because the region has just about everything for their pleasure and amusement. The Portuguese look after their own children and are pleased to see visitors taking the same attitude.

Modern hotels and apartments usually provide cots and high chairs for infants, but sometimes there is a small fee. Dried milk, disposable nappies and baby foods are obtainable at most supermarkets; plenty of toys and games are on sale, also beach wear and sports equipment. Playrooms, paddling pools and baby-sitting services (charges are about 500 escudos/£2 per hour) all help to make life easier for parents with small children. Package tour operators, such as Thomson Holidays, have hotels that specialise in catering for families with youngsters, offering children's menus and early suppers (see Chapter 4). Some hotels have Mini Clubs with staff who are trained to look after children. The cheery variety of programmes for the young are designed to entertain and amuse their junior members who are issued with a badge. Competitions are arranged so that parents can relax from their responsibilities for a while and have time to follow their own pursuits.

In the tourist resorts along the Algarve young children are allowed into bars, cafés, restaurants and hotel lounges until very late at night, even on to the dance floors. At Tom and Jerry's British Bar in Albufeira (next to the Bullring), children can enjoy special milk shakes, and cartoons are shown between 1400 and 1600 hrs. But it is worth remembering not to let your children become overtired. An afternoon or early evening rest is sensible, even if they protest and do not sleep, to prevent the child from getting exhausted.

Care should be taken even with teenagers that they do not have too much sunshine, especially during the first few days. The use of a sun barrier cream is helpful and a sun hat is recommended especially between noon and 1500 hrs, when the sun's rays are particularly strong during the summer months. With the excitement of the change of surroundings and different cooking, it is easy to be over indulgent. It is sensible to drink bottled water which is sold in supermarkets and hotels. Do wash all salads and fruit before eating. However nice the fresh peaches look on the market stall do not let children eat them without first washing them.

Young families can be taken on coach excursions and have a happy time, but remember to take some toys and games for little ones who can tire of looking at scenery. When the coach stops be sure to make use of the toilets, for it is not always possible for the driver to make extra stops along busy roads. For older children there are bicycles for hire and plenty of land and sea sports. Video games and discos are plentiful in the tourist resorts. Of course the greatest attraction is the lovely sandy beaches where safe swimming can be expected. However, on occasions a storm can blow up, so watch to see if a red flag is flying. This means rough seas and strong currents that make bathing dangerous, even for experienced swimmers.

Please do not force any child into the sea, it is so easy to make them afraid. Use a little encouragement by sitting at the water's edge and making a sand castle; then ask for some water for the moat. With patience the child will gain confidence and come to love being on the beach and, in time, going into the sea too.

Taking pets

If you wish to take your cat or dog with you to the Algarve, you will require a Health and Rabies Inoculation Certificate. You will need to enquire for this at the Portuguese National Tourist Office, New Bond Street House, 1-5 New Bond Street, London W1Y 0ND. Tel: 071-493 3873. Remember that on your return to the UK, your pet will have to spend six months in quarantine.

The larger supermarkets in the Algarve sell pet food. There is an English veterinary surgeon, Dr David G Hogger, with a clinic at Ladeira da Nora, Alvor, Portimão. Tel: 082 83656 (also residence).

The Arco da Vila is the main entrance to the old City of Faro,
conveniently alongside the Tourist Information Office, where you
can obtain a town map and other useful leaflets.

THREE

Getting there

By air

The Algarve's international airport is seven kilometres south west of the provincial capital, Faro. Because of the recent increase in the number of visitors flying to the Algarve, the airport has just opened a new terminal which almost doubles its capacity for handling passengers. The airport has the usual facilities of toilets, bar and restaurant open twenty-four hours, and luggage trolleys. There is a lost-and-found property office, a post office and a Tourist Information Office where they will also make accommodation reservations, as well as travel agents, bank and car rental firms, also newspapers and souvenir shop. Departing passengers may take advantage of a duty free shop when on international flights. For Faro airport information telephone 089 23081. The taxi fare from the airport to Faro city is 600 escudos (£2.40) and the bus fare 70 escudos (£0.28).

To get to the Algarve you can fly direct to Faro, or go to Lisbon airport and then on to Faro by air or road. Lisbon to Faro by road is 300kms (190 miles) on a surface that is mostly modern and good. There are express coaches. There is also a railway.

TAP (Air Portugal) is the national airline (tel: Faro 089 259808). The London Office is at 19 Regent Street, SW1 (tel: 071-828 0262). The return fare from London to Faro is currently £346. There are direct flights on Thursday, Saturday and Sunday taking about three hours. The daily flight between Lisbon and Faro takes about forty minutes.

British Airways (tel: 081-897 4000) also has scheduled flights daily, except on Tuesday, between London and Faro. Return fare Eurobudget costs £346.

Tour operators (see Chapter 2) have chartered aircraft that fly direct from Gatwick and other UK airports to Faro. Fares on charter flights can be considerably cheaper than on scheduled flights, depending on the time of year.

By road

To travel by road from the UK to the Algarve can be pleasant and interesting, provided you don't travel in the depths of winter. You have to decide which ports you wish to use.

Plymouth to Santander (Spain)

The quickest route is through Plymouth to Santander in northern Spain, and thence by road to Portugal. Brittany Ferries operate a regular vehicle and passenger ferry throughout the year. The crossing takes 24 hours in a fully stabilised and modern ship. Driving on to the car deck is a simple operation. The ship is comfortable with air conditioned two- and four-berth cabins, some having a shower and toilet. There are wide promenade sun decks, lounges with bars, restaurant and self-service cafeteria; dance floor, electronic games, shops, cinema, and children's room. One-way fare for two persons and car costs £203 to £259, depending on accommodation and season. Reservations can be made through travel agents or Brittany Ferries, Millbay Docks, Plymouth PL1 3EW. Tel: 0752 221321.

From Santander you take the N611 to Palencia and then the N620 to Valladolid, Salamanca, through Ciudad Rodrigo and across the frontier into Portugal, and the N16 to Guarda. From here the N17 leads to Coimbra where you turn south on the N1 towards Lisbon, which will be to the west as you continue south on the N10 through Alcácer do Sal, Grândola, Ovrique, and finally arriving on the Algarve at Albufeira. The total distance is about 700 miles (1120 kms) and the route is recommended as it is scenic and avoids high mountains. The road surfaces are better than others in central Portugal where they can be rough and cobbled.

There are various other routes, some being a little longer. From Santander you can go to Madrid and cross the frontier with Portugal at Badajoz; or from Madrid to Valdepeñas, Córdoba, Seville, Huelva and Ayamonte. Here you take your vehicle on the passenger ferry across to the Algarve at Vila Real de Santo António in the extreme south east of Portugal.

The frontier is open 0800 hrs until midnight (Spanish time). At Easter, Christmas and public holidays it is open twenty-four hours. The ferry service is frequent and it takes about twenty minutes to cross the estuary of the Rio Guadiana, which divides Spain from Portugal. The service is described more fully in the next section.

Via French ports

Brittany ferries also sail from Portsmouth to France, St Malo and Caen; from Poole to Cherbourg and Plymouth to Roscoff. Sealink and P & O Ferries will also take you across to France. The most direct route then would be to drive to Bordeaux and Biarritz, crossing into Spain at Hendaye and Irun. You then head for Vittoria, Burgos, Valladolid or Madrid, and on to Portugal.

By ferry

Although there are ports in the Algarve, cruise ships do not call, neither do any shipping companies bring passengers and vehicles.

However, there is a ferry between Spain and the Algarve, which crosses the wide estuary of the Rio Guadiana from Ayamonte in

One of the flat bottomed ferry boats that sail across the Rio Guadiana.

south west Spain to Vila Real de Santo António in the south east of Portugal. The Guadiana flows from north to south, forming the frontier between these two countries. The ferry service consists of three or four small, open deck, drive-on vehicle and passenger boats that operate throughout the year daily, during daylight hours, and they are always busy. Many visitors enter the Algarve this way, having driven from Seville, 160 kms (100 miles) and beyond. A great number of the passengers are day trippers making shopping expeditions or sightseeing, and the ferries are particularly busy at week-ends and on public holidays. It is not possible to make an advance booking, mainly because the boats do not run strictly to time. Ferries leave from either side every half hour and the crossing takes about twenty minutes. Tickets cost about 500 pesetas (£2.50) single for two adults and a car, or the equivalent in escudos. You just have to join the queue, which is quite orderly most of the time, though some confusion occurs if several tourist coaches arrive. Driving on to the ferry appears to be precarious, and you may have to do some reversing, but the crews are experienced and will assist you. There is little formality at either frontier. At Vila Real de Santo António there is a Tourist Information Office, currency exchange, shops and restaurants, most facilities being open on Sunday.

Construction has started on a new bridge over the Rio Guadiana, a few kilometres north of Vila Real de Santo Antonio. When completed, this should greatly increase the number of visitors using this route to the Algarve.

By coach

There are a number of coach services from London to Spain and Portugal. Travel Agents have information and can make reservations.

Euroways (52 Grosvenor Gardens, Victoria, London SW1. Tel: 071-730 8235) operate a service from London Victoria to Faro. During the summer, April to September, coaches leave on Saturday and Wednesday evenings. In winter it is once a week. The journey takes forty-eight hours and the adult fare is single £85, return £142.

By train

Information and tickets to travel by rail from the UK to the Algarve can be obtained from British Rail Continental Ltd., Ticket and Information Office, PO Box No 29, London SW1V 1JX (Tel: 071-834 2345) or train service information offices at main line railway stations and travel agents.

The train journey to the Algarve takes about thirty-six hours, going via a Channel port, Paris, Hendaye, the south-west frontier of France with Spain, then crossing the frontier in the north of Portugal and thence southwest to Lisbon. Another route goes via Madrid, crossing into Portugal at Valencia de Alcántara. There are special concessional fares for limited stays, young people and senior citizens.

Yacht facilities

Facilities for mooring private boats and yachts are found at Lagos, Portimão, Faro, Olhão and Sagres, which is still developing its new port.

At Vilamoura, near Quarteira and about half way between Faro and Albufeira, there is a full-scale marina with practically every facility possible for marinecraft. This is **Marina Vilamoura** (Tel: 089 32023. VHF Channel 62. Latitude 37° 04′4 N and longitude 8° 07′3 W). All jetties have water and electricity connections with telephones nearby. Refuelling can be done daily between 0930 and 1230 hrs and 1400 and 1900 hrs.

Mooring fees include water, electricity and other marina facilities. The fees vary according to length, beam, duration of stay and season. For example: a craft 6m long and 2.3m beam, for one day from May to December — 570 escudos (£2.29); a craft 15m long and 4.5m beam — 1,700 escudos (£6.80).

At Marina Vilamoura you will find ship's chandlers, supermarkets, restaurants and repair yards, slipway and gantry crane available, together with weather forecasts, charts, post office, telex and fax. Listening service VHF channel 16 & 62 (CB) channel 1 call signal Vilamoura Radio.

*The modern highrise hotels of Vilamoura stand out starkly on the
skyline. Seen here from the harbour of Quarteira.*

FOUR

Where to stay

The wide choice of accommodation in the Algarve ranges from five-star luxury hotels, family run hotels and simple hostels, to modern villas, high rise apartment blocks and camping parks. Because of the popularity of the Algarve it is advisable to reserve your accommodation, especially in July, August and early September.

In Portugal, all places of accommodation must by law exhibit their licence and tariff of charges. When you arrive at your destination you will receive a form which shows your room number, terms and date of arrival. You will also be required to hand in your passport for registration: it will be returned to you within twenty-four hours.

The star rating

Hotels and apartments throughout Portugal are officially inspected and classified with a one- to five-star rating, as used internationally.

Five-star hotel These are luxury hotels with every comfort in bedrooms and suites. Public rooms have a lavish decor and impeccable service. Amenities include high-class restaurants, grill room, comfortable lounges and often conference rooms. First-class swimming pools and sports facilities, hairdressing salon, sauna, fitness rooms are to be expected, with lifts to all floors. Evening entertainments, coach excursions, private beaches and beautiful surroundings are some of the things you expect in a five-star hotel.

Four-star hotel/apartment These are still quite luxurious and will have most of the features mentioned above, but they will cost less and the decor and location may not be so impressive.

Three-star hotel/apartment These will lack amenities and the public areas may not be so spacious, with the decor and service being less elaborate, but they should be clean and comfortable.

Two and one-star hotel/apartment These provide simple accommodation, usually of the commercial type. They may not have a swimming pool or a lift, but they should be clean and friendly.

In the Algarve there are several other types of accommodation, also regulated by the government. A 'turistic' village complex has villas and apartments rated up to three stars, with a top luxury classification. An *estalgem* (inn) is usually in the country and smaller than a hotel in the same class. A *pensao* (pension) is a boarding house, usually with simple, clean and inexpensive rooms. Sometimes breakfast is provided but there will be no restaurant service. *O turismo de habitacao* is a country house, manor or castle that has been opened by the owner for public use. Usually they are of a high standard. *Albergarias* are good quality inns, sometimes old buildings, which do not have full hotel facilities.

State run hotels are called *pousadas* (similar to the Spanish *paradores);* they are often in out-of-the-way but pleasing locations. *Pousadas* were inaugurated in 1940 by the late Antonio d'Oliveira Salazar, Portugal's dictator, when he felt that there was a requirement for modern accommodation for tourists. Castles, mansions and new buildings were fitted out in a regional style and deliberately kept small so that guests could meet fellow travellers in a friendly and comfortable atmosphere. If you require more information about *pousadas,* you can write, or make a reservation through Enatur, Avenida Santa Joana Princesa 10, Lisbon 1700. Tel: 01 881221/889078. Telex 13690.

Hotels

A complete list of places offering accommodation in the Algarve can be obtained from the Portuguese National Tourist Office, New Bond Street House, 1-5 New Bond Street, London W1Y 0NP. Tel: 071-493 3873. Travel agents will be able to advise you about package holiday accommodation. We are including here a list of the more popular hotels, apartments and holiday villages. For easy location on a map of the Algarve, towns are listed in an east to west direction which matches our description of tours in Chapters 10 to 13. Under each town, accommodation is listed alphabetically under star order.

Vila Real de Santo António

Apola (three-star) Rua Bombeiros, Tel: 44448/9. 42 rooms with balcony. Recently built at back of town near fire station. Restaurant for groups only.

Monte Gordo

Alcazar (four-star) Rua de Ceuta, Tel: 42184. 95 rooms and suites. Radio and telephone. Air-conditioned. Well established. In side road ten minutes from beach. Quiet, friendly atmosphere.

Casablanca Inn (four-star) Rua 7, Tel: 42444. 46 rooms. Quiet, small and friendly, easy walk to beach and shops. Recommended.

Vasco da Gama (four-star) Ave. Infante D Henrique, Tel: 44321. 200 rooms and suites. Radio and telephone. Well appointed and good for sports and dancing. Right on beach.

Das Caravelas (three-star) Rua Diogo Cao, Tel: 44458. 90 rooms with telephone. Guests may use facilities of Hotel Vasco da Gama. Five minutes from beach.

Dos Navegadores (three-star) Rua Concalves Velho, Tel: 42490. 356 rooms. Telephone and central heating. Indoor pool, roof top sunterrace, disco. Cheerful and good for families. Situated at back of town. Recommended.

Albergaria Monte Gordo (four-star *albergaria)* Ave. Infante D Henrique, Tel: 42124. 49 rooms. American operated. Special off-season rates. Bar with music. No swimming pool. Quiet. Five minutes from beach.

Tavira

Hotel Apartments Eurotel Altura (three-star) Quinta Das Oliveiras, Tel: 95450. 135 rooms, all facing sea. Balcony, radio and telephone. Supermarket, outdoor pool, playground, disco. Isolated position on beach, between Monte Gordo and Tavira. Good for windsurfing. Suitable for young families.

Hotel Apartments, Eurotel Tavira (three-star) Quinta Das Oliveiras, Tel: 22041. 80 rooms. Pool, playground and disco. In countryside on main road. Same management as Hotel Altura.

Faro

Eva (four-star) Ave Da Republica, Tel: 24054. 138 rooms, 12 suites. Central heating. Modern hotel close to city centre overlooking yacht harbour. Roof restaurant. Adult and children's pool, disco and night club.

Riamar (four-star) Praia de Faro, Tel: 23542. 20 rooms. South of airport by beach. Tourist Office recommended.

Faro (three-star) Dr D Francisco Gomes, Tel: 22076. 44 rooms including suites. Roof top sun deck. In city centre. Portuguese operated.

Albacor (two-star) Rua Brites de Almeida 23-25, Tel: 22093. 38 rooms. Bar, lounge, no dining room. In old part of city (but not through Arco da Vila).

Garantia (Apartments Tourist) Rua Cons. Bivar, Tel: 24087. 23 penthouse apartments, fully furnished, TV, radio. Maid service. In city, by seafront.

Casade Lumana (three-star pension) Praça Alexanddra Herlulano 7, Tel: 22028. 11 rooms with bath. Restaurant and bar. In city square. English managed.

O'Farao (3 star pension) Largo da Madalena 4, Tel: 23356. 23 rooms with bath. Restaurant. In city near shops.

Almancil
Quinta do Lago (five-star) Tel: 96666. 150 rooms and suites. Air-conditioned. Satellite TV. Super luxury hotel belonging to the Orient Express. Set in 1,600 acres of pinewoods, sandy beach, fabulous sports facilities. Windsurfing on inland lake. Heated pool. Championship golf. Secretarial services. Half an hour from airport.

Hotel Apartments La Reserve (four-star) St Barbara de Nexe, Tel: 91234. 20 suites with terrace, sea view. Small, luxury, country hotel. Highclass restaurant. Member Reláis and Chateau.

Vale do Lobo
Dona Filipa (five-star) Tel: 94141. 135 rooms with balcony, air-conditioned. Pinewood setting, exclusive, well established. Elegant and peaceful. Golf. Close to beach. Trusthouse Forte owned. Twenty minutes from airport.

Quarteira
Hotel Apartments Quarteirasol (four-star) Praia da Quarteira, Tel: 34421. 110 rooms. 275 apartments. Sol complex, 100m from sea. Plenty of amusements for a family holiday.

Dom Jose (three-star) Ave. Infante de Sagres, Tel: 34310. 134 rooms. Modern, comfortable, functional family hotel on beach. Free cots. Disco.

Vilamoura

Atlantis (five-star) Tel: 32535. 305 rooms, seaview. 14 storey, de luxe, ultra modern hotels overlooking yacht marina. The Health centre, sports facilities, golf courses, international atmosphere.

Vilamoura Marina (five-star) Tel: 33310. 388 rooms and suites. Large, luxury, modern hotel, right by yacht marina. Sophisticated clientele. Conference rooms. Health club, massage. Many water sports facilities.

Dom Pedro (four-star) Tel: 35450. 260 rooms. Balcony, telephone, air-conditioned. New and modern. Short distance from sandy beach, close to yacht marina and shops.

Albufeira

Balaia (five-star) Praia Maria Luish, Tel: 52681. 187 rooms, 6 suites. Select luxury hotel with plenty of sports, entertainment and nightclub. Five kilometres east of Albufeira in forty acres, cliff top setting, own beach.

Montechoro (four-star) San João, Tel: 52651. 362 rooms, 48 suites. One of the largest hotels with first-class facilities. Conference rooms. All year entertainment, sports, gymnasium. Special features for children. Courtesy bus to nearby beach. Set in busy tourist area.

Solemar (four-star) Tel: 52121. 68 rooms. Good position on seafront and by town and shops. Early suppers for children. Pool not suitable for children, but lovely beach down steps. Disco in season.

Vila Recife (three-star *pensão*) Rua Miguel Bornbarda 6, Tel: 52047. 95 rooms. Once a villa, this small hotel has a highly individual atmosphere. Close to shops and beach. Use of facilities in Hotel Solymar. Friendly attentive staff.

Almacão de Pera

Garbe (four-star) Tel: 32187. 90 rooms, 11 suites. Good reputation. On cliffs with direct access to beach. Swimming pool built into cliffs.

Casa Bela Moura *(pensão)* Alporchinos, Tel: 33422. 2 apartments, 10 rooms with bath. Country inn with garden, small pool and bar. Nearby restaurant.

Praia da Rocha

Algarve (five-star) Tel: 24001. 220 rooms, 12 yachting suites, 3 de luxe suites. On beach. Air-conditioned. Moorish decor. Grill room. Plenty of entertainment, nightclub and floorshow.

Bela Vista (four-star) Tel: 24055. 14 rooms, 2 suites with mini bar and TV. Unique old palace with antique decor. Quiet. Beach setting. Recommended.
Da Rocha (three-star) Avenida Thomas Cabreira, Tel: 24081. 77 rooms. Well established. Families with children welcome. By beach and shops. Shares facilities with nearby Da Rocha 2.

Portimão
Alvor Praia (five-star) Praia dos Tres Irmaos, Tel: 24021. 241 rooms, air-conditioned. Luxury hotel overlooking splendid beach. Conference and banquet rooms. International menu. Plenty of sports, shop, entertainments.
Dennis Inn Rua 5 de Outubro, Tel: 24273. 6 rooms. Old Portuguese inn, near town centre and parish church. Beautiful rooms. Pretty courtyard. Evening barbecue.

Alvor
Dom João 11 (four-star) Tel: 20135. 220 rooms, 18 suites. Modern, well appointed with all facilities, central heating. Portuguese decor. By sandy beach and Penina golf course. Early suppers for children.
Delfim (four-star) Tel: 27171. 325 rooms. High rise hotel by beach. Well appointed with all facilities. Central heating. All meals buffet style. Relaxed holiday atmosphere. Children's entertainments.

Penina
Penina Golf (five-star) Tel: 22051. 200 rooms and 14 suites, air-conditioned. Well established Trusthouse Forte. Elegant, secluded garden setting. Henry Cotton golf course. Excellent grill room. Conference rooms, sports. Bus to private beach. Special entertainments for children. Casino nearby. Friendly relaxed atmosphere. Well recommended.

Lagos
Hotel de Lagos (four-star) Tel: 62011. 287 rooms, 11 suites, air-conditioned, balconies. On hill in town. Private beach club. Sports, indoor pool. Spacious, comfortable, well appointed, friendly staff. Conference rooms. Recommended.
Sol A Sol (three star *pensão*) Rua Lancerote de Freitas, Tel: 62190. 15 rooms. Clean, simple and friendly. By bus station.

Monchique
Abrigo da Montanha (four-star *estalagem*) Estrada de Fóia, Tel: 92131. 6 rooms with bath.

Albergaria Lageado (four-star *albergaria*) Caldas de Monchique, Tel: 92203. 21 rooms. Beautiful old inn near the 'waters'. Lush vegetation in quiet valley. recommended.

Pousadas

Pousada do Infante Sagres, Tel: 64222. 21 rooms, with balcony overlooking the sea. Well established. Splendid cliff top position, attractive Portuguese decor. Log fire in winter. Varied menu in excellent restaurant. Recommended.

Pousada São Bras de Alportel Tel: 42305. 45 rooms. Attractive building overlooking town and hills. Well maintained. Peaceful setting, pretty garden. Recommended.

Camping and campsites

The Algarve region of Portugal is one of the most popular places for camping, offering fine stretches of sandy beaches, many flat roads and a comparatively safe, peaceful way of life. Caravanners and tenters feel they can relax and enjoy the pleasant climate. Portuguese people themselves own caravans and many who live in big cities like to leave their mobile home in the Algarve, so often a large proportion of a camping park is occupied by Portuguese units. A booklet and map containing details of officially classified sites is produced by Direcção General do Turismo (Palácio Foz. Praça dos Restauradores, Lisbon. Tel: 36 70 31); or apply to the Portuguese National Tourist Office (New Bond Street House, 1-5 New Bond Street, London W1Y 0NP. Tel: 071-493 3873). Available at some tourist offices and campsites, the camping guide book, *Roteiro Campista,* lists all the 146 sites in Portugal.

Generally speaking, the campsites in the Algarve are of a good standard, clean and friendly. They vary from the simple to vast recreational parks. The charges are usually lower than in the rest of Europe, and discounts are given for long stay campers during the winter. In the busy summer months it is necessary to book your pitch in advance. Limited camping outside recognised sites is permitted but not advisable. Overnight stops in parking and rest areas are not allowed.

It is well to remember that in summer the mid-day temperatures can be very high, so a flysheet, awning or sunshade is advantageous.

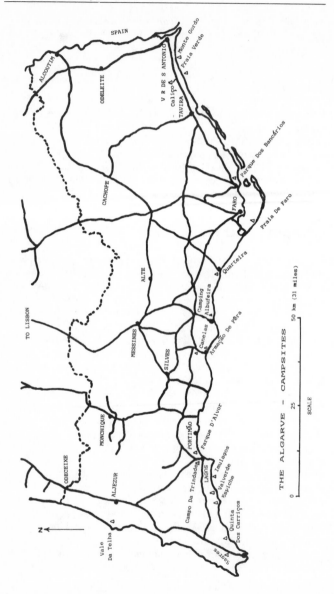

THE ALGARVE - CAMPSITES

During winter strong winds can blow and rain may be heavy. Spring and autumn are particularly pleasant for camping and touring. The roads along the coast are suitable for caravans but some in the mountains are not. The Caravan Club's Red Pennant service supply an overseas map that shows roads suitable for caravans.

On arrival at a campsite you must produce your passport and some require a Camping Carnet (obtained from the AA, RAC, Caravan Club, or Camping and Caravanning Club.

Camping parks are given an official one to four star rating according to facilities, four stars being the highest. Prices vary according to the season. High season is usually July and August, mid June, September and October, the rest of the year being low season. All the campsites listed here are open throughout the year and have hot showers and electric hookups. A refill 907 cylinder of Camping Gaz costs 525 escudos (£2.10) and is readily available in the Algarve (but not always on camping parks).

Prices quoted here are per night and average, but tend to increase each year. Discounts for long stays are usually given.

- Adult — 70 to 320 escudos (£0.28 to £1.28)
- Child — 50 to 160 escudos (£0.20 to £0.64)
- Car — 50 to 200 escudos (£0.20 to £0.80)
- Caravan — 95 to 340 escudos (£0.38 to £1.36)
- Motorhome — 105 to 300 escudos (£0.42 to £1.20)
- Small tent — 90 to 190 escudos (£0.36 to £0.76)
- Large tent — 125 to 270 escudos (£0.50 to £1.08)
- Motorcycle — 60 to 160 escudos (£0.24 to £0.64)
- Electricity — 50 to 150 escudos (£0.20 to £0.60). Can be inclusive.

Monte Gordo

Municipal de Campismo Monte Gordo (two-star) Vila Real de Santo António, Tel: 42588. Capacity 2,500 persons. Situated 4km west of Vila Real de Santo António on the main route to Faro. An extensive camp in sandy woodlands, opposite a golden beach, close to the frontier with Spain. In summer it has a high percentage of Spanish campers; winter sees a big influx of German and British, some spend the whole winter on this camp. From November to March there is a 30 per cent reduction on production of a Camping Carnet. Facilities are clean but not very modern. Large grocery store, newspaper and gift shop, restaurant (in season). Five-minute walk to centre of Monte Gordo, 40-minute level walk to Vila Real de Santo António.

Campismo Torralta Praia Verde (two-star) Tel: 42382. Capacity 5,000 persons. Situated in sandy pinewoods by beach 4km west of Monte Gordo, just off the main route Faro to Vila Real de Santo António. Well organised high-price camp, with large proportion of German campers. A reduction of 10 per cent for a 30-day stay from October to April. Usually fully booked during July and August. Restaurant (overlooking beach), cafeteria, bar, post office and supermarket, all open all year. Tennis courts.

Calico

Campismo Vila Nova de Cacela (one-star) Trascampo — Sociedade Imobiliaria, Tel: 95195. Capacity 300 persons. Situated 2km north of Cacela, in a quiet rural setting away from the tourist areas, with modern toilet facilities and a swimming pool. It is Camping and Caravanning Club recommended. Children under four years free; 15 per cent discount for a 60-day stay, 10 per cent discount for 30-days. Supermarket, children's playground, restaurant (in season). Good beach at Manta Rota (5km).

Olhão

Parque dos Bancarios (three-star) Pinheiros de Marim, Tel: 75102. Capacity 3,000 persons. Situated 1km east of Olhão, close to pinewoods and sandy beach. A modern site recently opened and nicely planned, with good toilet blocks and large supermarket. Tennis courts, swimming pool, children's playground, restaurant.

Faro

Camara Municipal de Faro Praia de Faro. Tel: 24876. The camp is situated 8km south of Faro, past the airport and across causeway, on level, sandy ground, opposite sand dunes and extensive beach. There are many Portuguese caravans and holiday homes. Bus route a short distance from entrance. Some noise from aircraft. Modern toilet facilities. Supermarket, small playground. No restaurant.

Quarteira

Camping Orbitur (three-star) Tel: 35238. Capacity 1,350 persons. Located on the outskirts of Quarteira and set in dense pinewoods, 500m from the sea. This undulating camp contains many Portuguese caravans and has A-frame bungalows for hire. Discount given from October to May. Large supermarket, restaurant. Facilities for the disabled.

Albufeira
Camping Albufeira (three-star) Rocha-Mar, Sarl, Tel: 53853. Capacity 3,000 persons. Situated inland between the EN125 Portimão to Faro road and the EN526 Almacoa to Balaia road. This large modern camping park is well organised, with many good facilities. Five sandy beaches within an 8km radius. There is a 30 per cent discount from November to 16 April. Large supermarket, bars, self-service restaurant, disco, sun terrace, heated swimming pool, waterslide, TV room, children's playground.

Armação de Pera
Parque de Campismo (two-star) Praia de Armação de Pera, Tel: 32260. Capacity 500 persons. Situated 300m from the sea, south of the EN125. This mainly level site is popular with British long-stay campers during the winter months. There is a 50 per cent discount from October to May. Beach and town 15-minute walk away. A good supermarket and clubhouse, with TV. In the high season a restaurant and snack bar.

Parque de Campismo (three-star) Turismovel — Soc. de Turismo do Algarve, Canelas, Tel: 32612. Capacity 900 persons. Just 1km from the sea, on the EN269. This large camp has many Portuguese caravans on site. It is clean with many facilities. There is 15 per cent discount on production of a Camping Carnet. Supermarket and restaurant in season. Children's playground, tennis courts, beach/town 15-minute walk.

Alvor
Parque D'Alvor (one-star) Tel: 20178. Capacity 600 persons. Situated close to the village in a rural setting, this small park has been open for ten years, so fitments are no longer new. ADAC and ACSI listed. There is a bar and friendly atmosphere but the site is not very level. A 25 per cent discount is given October to May. Supermarket and restaurant when camp is busy.

Lagos
Campo da Trindade (one-star) Club de Futebol Esperanca, Tel: 62913. Capacity 250. Situated close to the football stadium, at the western end of Lagos, on a hill. This small site is a ten-minute walk downhill to the centre of town and quite a climb on the way back. Often crowded it is only useful for a short stay. Discount of 25 per cent November to April. Supermarket, restaurant (in season).

Parque de Campismo de Lagos (three-star) Estrada Porto de Mos, Imulgos, Tel: 60031. Capacity 3,000 persons. Situated on the western outskirts of Lagos. This is a very large camping park, spread out generously with trees and flowering shrubs. It lies on a cliff top with steep steps to a secluded beach. Toilet blocks and all facilities are in good order. Restaurant, bar and disco during high season. Large supermarket, post office, telephones, playground, tennis courts, swimming pool.

The Parque de Campismo de Lagos, has plenty of trees providing shade.

Valverde Campismo (four-star) Rotasol Emp. de Turismo do Algarve, Praia da Luz, Tel: 69211. Capacity 1,500. On the left-hand side of the road, 1.5km from Praia da Luz. Well established trees give shade. This first class campsite has facilities for the disabled. Quiet during winter, in summer there is plenty of on site entertainment. Large supermarket (open all year), restaurant and take-away (in season). Playground, tennis courts, swimming pool, TV room, disco, post office, telephone and telex facilities. No dogs.

Turiscampo Loa (one-star) Espiche, Tel: 69431. Capacity 1,000 persons. This park is on the main EN125, 4km west of Lagos and 2km from Praia da Luz beach. On a bus route, it is a useful park for visiting Lagos. Some noise from passing traffic. Playground, supermarket, restaurant.

Praia de Salema

Quinta dos Carricos (one-star) Tel: 65201. Capacity 350 persons. a small camp within walking distance of Praia de Salema, 1km to the south. It is just off the EN125, between Lagos and Figueira. This park has toilet facilities for wheelchair-bound campers. Supermarket, restaurant, post office.

Sagres

Soporim Loa (one-star) Tel: 64361. Capacity 1,000. Situated just off the EN268, Vila do Bispo to Sagres road. The entrance is down an unmade road and, as yet, this site is not fully developed. It can be windy here. There is a 20 per cent discount from October to May. Supermarket and restaurant in season.

Aljezur

Vale de Telha (three-star) Praia Monte Clerigo, Tel: 72444. Capacity 1,500 persons. This is a splendid camping park, off the beaten track on the western Algarve coast, close to unspoilt, wild sandy beaches, good for windsurfing. Modern toilet block and well stocked supermarket. Quiet in winter; during the summer, there's a disco, restaurant, barbecue, tennis and squash. Children's playground.

Time share

Purchasing a time share in property is an option for those who want to spend their holidays in their own place in the Algarve. There are a number of companies offering villas, such as the **Four Seasons Country Club** (Quinta do Lago) which offers weekly ownership from £3,900 of apartments, including many social and recreational facilities. Details can be obtained from Apt. 58. 8106 Almancil Codex. Tel: 089 94326 or 140 Tabernacle Street, London EC2A 4SD. Tel: 01-251 1046. Another such company is the Impervilla Holiday Club, Vilamoura. Tel: 089 35372.

Your own property

The Algarve presents an appealing location for purchasers to invest in property. Many British people have owned property here for a long time and are accepted into the local community. It is advisable to get specialist advice on the subject, because the Portuguese methods of property transaction differ from those in the UK.

The selling of apartments and villas, the administration of property, letting, legal advice, repairs, technical services and insurance are carried out by real estate companies in the Algarve and Portugal, some with connections in the UK. Many of the firms employ English-speaking staff trained to assist clients from abroad. Some estate agents in the Algarve are:

Villas and Homes Head Office: Estrada Nacional 125, Almancil, 8100, Loulé. Tel: 089 95435. London Office: 113 Baker Street, W1M 1FE. Tel: 071-487 5868.

Tanfield Rua Dr João Vitorina Mealha 26, Portimão. Tel: 082 25469.

Iberus Avenida 25 de Abril 5, Albufeira. Tel: 089 54416. UK Address: Housman, 7 Main Road, Hockley, Essex SS5 4QY. Tel: 0702 206281

There are English speaking solicitors experienced in all aspects of property sales and purchases throughout the Algarve. The names of three are given here:

Dr Rui Avelar Rua João da Cruz, Portimão. Tel: 082 26162

Dr Conceição Silva Rua Conselheiro J Machado 37, Lagos. Tel: 082 60420.

Dr Luis Galvão Rue de Santo António 68, Faro. Tel: 89 23099.

Removals

A company which handles removals between the UK and Portugal is **Robert Darvall Ltd,** 4 Acre Road, Reading, Berks, RG2 0SK. Tel: 0734 864422. They also have an office in the Algarve, at Rua Judice Fialho 15a, 8500 Portimão. Tel: 082 23508.

FIVE

Getting about the Algarve

The EN125 is the main road through the Algarve. It runs a little inland from the coast, westwards from Vila Real de Santo António and Monte Gordo to Tavira, Olhão, Faro, Almancil; then north of Albufeira and continuing westwards to Portimão, Lagos and Vila do Bispo. Here it joins the N268 which runs south to Sagres and north to Aljezur.

The EN125 is generally quite a good road with some dual carriageway, and there are some SOS telephones for use in an emergency. Work is going on to improve the bypass towns like Portimão and Faro. A good bus service covers the whole of the coastal length of the Algarve. Taxis are used a great deal, as are bicycles because there are few hills along the EN125.

A railway runs between Lagos and Vila Real de Santo António. Stations are sometimes some distance from towns and are connected by a bus service or taxi. The railway station serving Albufeira is at Ferreiras.

Walking is a very popular and satisfactory way of seeing the country and mountains. A map of Portugal is useful and a good one that includes the Algarve is published by Roger Lascelles, Cartographic and Travel Publisher, 47 York Road, Brentford, Middlesex, TW8 0QP. Tel: 081-847 0935 (Portugal Sheets 9/10. 1:300,000. Price £3.95).

Driving in Portugal

If you are taking a car to the Algarve and driving through France and Spain you will require the following:

1 Driving Licence.
2 International Driving Permit (from the AA or RAC).
3 Green Card Insurance (issued by your insurance company).

4 Bail Bond (for Spain), from the AA, RAC or insurance company. This is an indemnity if you are involved in an accident.
5 Vehicle Registration Document.
6 Passport.
7 A spare set of vehicle light bulbs (a Spanish law requirement).
8 A red triangle, for warning of breakdown obstruction.
9 Means of changing direction of headlight dip.
10 GB sticker.

Up-to-date information about driving is best obtained from the AA, RAC, Spanish and Portuguese Tourist Offices. However, you need to be aware of the following important points:

● Drive on the right-hand side of the road
● Sound horn when overtaking
● Stop for pedestrians on crossings
● Wear seat belts
● Side lights only in built-up areas
● Do not cross a single white line (which is equivalent to the double white line in the UK)
● Observe 'no overtaking' signs and speed limits
● Give way to traffic coming from the right, particularly at roundabouts
● It is forbidden to carry petrol in cans in a vehicle
● Do not park facing on-coming traffic

Road signs

International road signs are used in the Algarve. In addition, some notices are written in Portuguese. Some important ones to remember are:

Alto	Halt
Encruzilhada/cruzamento	Crossroads
Perigo/perigosa	Danger
Descida ingreme	Steep hill
Desvio	Diversion
Paragem	Bus stop
Pare	Stop
Passagem proíbida/ Sentido proíbida	No entry
Sem Saida	No through road

Petrol stations

The Algarve is well served for petrol filling stations. They are to be found mostly on the EN125, the main road that runs east to west. They are modern and a number accept credit cards. Some are open twenty-four hours and on Sunday. Generally they do not provide repair services. There are autoshops that sell spares, sweets and drinks and sometimes there are toilets. Car wash services are similar to those in the UK. Petrol comes in two grades, Super 96 octane and Normal which is only 90 octane and is not suitable for most modern cars. Diesel fuel is also available. At the time of writing, diesel is £1.28 a gallon and Super petrol £2.20 a gallon. Petrol is *gasolina* and diesel is *gasóleo*. Unleaded petrol is not yet generally available.

Car servicing and repairs

There are numerous places for servicing and repairing cars and there are many cars of British and foreign makes to be seen on the roads in the Algarve. In Faro there are agents for most well known vehicles, though there could be some delay in obtaining a particular spare from abroad. It is advisable to take out vehicle security insurance with a motoring organisation like the AA or RAC before leaving the UK. If you belong to one of these you can make use of the Automóvel Clube de Portugal for free emergency service. They have breakdown garages in Faro, Lagos and Portimão. You ask for a *mechânico automóveis* if you require a motor mechanic.

Self drive car rental

There are many car rental firms in the Algarve. (Some like Europcar will provide drivers.) This is the way to see the country and of course, you can travel further into Portugal. It is advisable to book your vehicle a few days in advance to avoid disappointment. The cost includes third party insurance and unlimited kilometres. It does not include cost of fuel, nor personal or collision insurance, for which you pay extra as optional. To cover the driver and all passengers costs about 250 escudos (£1) a day. The minimum age for self-drive hire is 21, with at least one year's driving experience. A valid driving licence or international driving permit is required to be produced.

Naturally, rental charges vary with the type of car you hire but expect to pay something in the region of the following: Opel Corsa — 2200 escudos (£8.80); Ford Escort — 2900 escudos (£11.60); Renault Trafic diesel — 6000 escudos (£24); Volvo 240 GLE — 9500 escudos (£38).

A deposit is usually requested in the region of 30,000 escudos (£120), or payment in advance. International credit cards (Visa and Access) are accepted for payment.

You can arrange with Avis in the UK to have a car to meet you at Faro Airport. Telephone 'Avis Drive Away', 081-848 8733. Car rentals in the Algarve can be arranged through travel agents, hotel receptions and at the airport at Faro. Telephone numbers of some of the firms which operate are:

Avis Faro Airport, 089 22085

Budget Rent-a-Car Faro (Eva Hotel) 089 271100; Albufeira, 089 54997; Monte Gordo, 081 44458; Praia da Rocha, 082 22370; Quarteira, 089 33046.

Europcar Faro Airport, 089 23777.

Hertz Faro Airport, 089 24048; Vilamoura, Aldeia do Mar, 089 35185.

Kenning Faro Airport, 089 20251.

Scooters, mopeds and motorcycles

You can hire various types of scooter, moped or motor cycle on a daily basis or weekly basis. The distance allowed is usually unlimited and insurance is arranged. Two places where this can be done, amongst the many, are the **Tavira Rent-a-Bike,** Rua da Porta Nova, Tavira. Tel: 081 23661; and **Scooterent,** Rua Afonso D'Almeida 15, Lagos. Tel: 082 62903.

Taxis

The taxis in the Algarve are black with a green roof. A large letter 'A' is marked on the doors.

Taxis are quite numerous, they are clean and generally give a good service. Compared with prices in Europe the fares are quite cheap. In the Algarve taxis do not have meters, but there is a fare tariff based on distance. It is advisable to agree the price before getting into the vehicle. The fare will be the same however many people use the taxi. If you are the only passenger the driver will expect you to sit next to him. Taxi drivers expect to receive a tip in the region of ten per cent of the fare.

You will need to telephone or order your taxi from the hotel porter, otherwise go to a taxi rank. It is not usually possible to engage a passing taxi. To call a taxi telephone: Lagos 082 63587/62239; Alvor 082 20695; Portimão 082 23615/23317; Lagoa 082 52556; Albufeira 089 52227; Faro 089 23537; Tavira 081 22439/22704; Vila Real de Santo de António 081 44444/44525; Loulé 089 62601.

Buses

The bus service in the Algarve is called the Rodoviaria Nacional (RN), it is also the national service of Portugal. The main bus station, where all journeys originate, is in the centre of Faro, Avenida Dom Infant Henriques 76. This is on the seafront and close to the railway station *(caminhos de ferro).*

The cheapest way to travel in Portugal is by bus and these will take you nearly everywhere in the country. There are good express and normal services between Vila Real de Santo António, the eastern frontier of the Algarve, and the capital, Faro. You would then need to change buses to continue, by express, to Sagres, the furthest place in the south west.

Bus stops are signed *paragem.* Some buses board at the rear, but the doors should be marked *entrada* (entrance) or *saída* (exit). Depending on the service, you pay on entering the bus or wait until your fare is collected. You can buy your ticket at a bus station prior to your journey. This must be done if you are taking an express bus.

Railways

There is a very good railway network covering most of Portugal. It has first- and second-class carriages. On the long distance services there are restaurant cars (but not in the Algarve). Cars are accepted on most trains, but fifteen days notice must be given to the station of departure. Further information on the Portuguese Railways *(caminhos de ferro)* can be obtained from Santa Apolónia, Lisbon 1200, or from travel agents in the UK.

In the Algarve, the railway runs from Vila Real de Santo António to Lagos, with stations at Cacela, Tavira, Fuseta, Olhão, Faro,

Loulé, Albufeira (although the station is actually near Ferreiras, about fifteen minutes by bus from the resort), Tunes, Alcantarilha, Silves, Estômber and Portimão. It is essential you purchase a ticket before boarding the train, otherwise a fine has to be paid.

There is not much difference in cost of long distance travel between buses and trains, but you will probably see more of the country by train. The junction for a train from the Algarve to Lisbon is at Tunes; an express will take about three hours to Barreiro; there you board a ferry to cross the Rio Tagus into Lisbon.

Behind the fish market at Olhãu, this patient mule awaits his owner's return. Note the line of octopus on the poles.

Horse-drawn carriages

Horse-drawn carriages *(carrinhas)* are to be found in Vila Real de Santo António, Monte Gordo, Quarteria and Praia da Rocha. They are a popular tourist attraction and nowadays special excursion rides take visitors into the countryside.

In general these two-wheel carriages, sometimes called 'buggies', seat four people, although there is room for an extra person up front with the driver. A leather hood or sunshade can be used when it is raining, windy or too hot. Sometimes a mule will be pulling the carriage. Always the animal will wear an ornate harness, decorated with bells and coloured tassels and blinkers. Should your journey take you up a steep hill, the men and stout persons may be requested to alight and walk.

Having a carriage ride is a pleasant and relaxing way to do your sight-seeing. Often your driver will enliven the journey with information and, sometimes, funny stories. However, it is wise to agree the fare before you start the ride.

Excursions

Most of the hotels arrange coach excursions and tour representatives will be eager to explain to you the various places that can be visited. When your holiday is for a limited period, or if you do not wish to rent a car, then the easiest way to enjoy the sights of the Algarve is to join a coach excursion. Half day, whole day and evening trips can be booked, even visits as far away as Seville, Lisbon and Morocco.

You may wish to make sure that your coach has an English-speaking guide and to check if the cost covers a meal. Remember to take sunglasses, a hat and camera, also a towel if a visit to a beach is included. Flat shoes are always more comfortable as you will be climbing in and out of the coach quite often. Your tour is likely to stop at souvenir shops, so some extra escudos may be required. It is normal practice to tip the coach driver about 150 escudos at the end of the excursion. You will feel it is worth it after you have experienced some of the narrow roads and difficult parking places.

As well as coach excursions there are buggy rides, which take you in a horse drawn carriage to visit a nature reserve and castle. This is a delightful experience, jogging along at a slow pace in the pretty countryside, but the men may need to get out and walk a little when going up hill!

River and fishing trips are popular. They are usually a full day outing and include freshly caught fish for your lunch.

Parties at restaurants, nightclubs, barbecues and the casino make pleasant evening excursions.

A full day coach ride from Monte Gordo to Sagres, driving along the length of the Algarve and back, will necessitate your starting at 0830 hrs and returning about 2030 hrs. The cost is about 4,500 escudos (£18) with half price for children. The buggy ride, including lunch, is about 3,000 escudos (£12), and the river trip 4,100 escudos (£16.40). Many of the excursions can be booked at a travel agent.

Many churches in the Algarve contain wonderful pictures of historical scenes, created in the beautiful blue and white, azulejos tiles.

SIX

A-Z information for visitors

British Consul

If anything untoward should happen, like losing your passport, it
is useful to know the whereabouts of the British Consul in the
Algarve. The office of the British Consul in Portimão is at 21 Rua
de Santa Isabel. Tel: 082 23071 and 27057 (Consulada Britânico:
Senhor José Manuel Pearce de Azevedo).

Churches

The Portuguese are mostly Roman Catholics and have many
churches in towns and villages. Visitors are always welcomed with
courtesy, when appropriately dressed. Mass can also be heard in
English in some Roman Catholic churches.

Anglican and Evangelical Church services are held in tourist
resorts, usually in Roman Catholic Churches. Details are given in
the English newspaper *Algarve News,* published fortnightly, and are
also available from tourist offices and hotels. The Reverend Canon
Douglas Ward Boddington (Casa Raquel Boliqueime, 8100, Loulé.
Tel: 089 66720) is the resident Chaplain, St Mary's Church,
Vilamoura.

Communications

Post

There are post offices in all the towns and some villages. Mobile
post offices are to be seen in the country. Visitors can have their
mail sent to main post offices for collection. It should be addressed
with the surname first, followed by Posta Restante and the name of
the town. To collect mail addressed to you, you must show your

passport as a means of identification. The post offices in Faro, Lagos, Portimão, Olhão, Tavira, Vila Real de Santo António, Albufeira and Conceicão are open Monday to Friday from 0900 to 1900 hrs. In Fuseta, Luz, Vila Nova de Cacela, Monte Gordo, Armação de Pera, Vilamoura, Almancil, Praia da Luz, Sagres and Vila do Bispo, opening hours are Monday to Friday 0900 to 1230 and 1400 to 1800 hrs. The main post office in Faro is also open on Saturday from 0900 to 1200 hrs.

At the time of writing, postage to the UK costs 60 escudos (£0.24) for a letter and 55 escudos (£0.22) for a postcard. Stamps *(selos)* can also be purchased at hotel receptions, tobacconists and some shops. All lightweight mail goes by air and can be registered. Post offices are indicated by the letters C.T.T. (Correios, Telegrafos e Telefones). Letter posting boxes follow the British design and are painted red.

Telephones

In towns automatic telephones *(telefone)* are to be found on the streets, in bars, restaurants and at post offices. For a call use a 2, 10, 20 or 25 escudo coin. Add more if your call is to be lengthy as unused coins are returned. Recently Credifone cards have been introduced. These are available from a post office in units of 25 to 1000 escudos. Telephones in bars are usually metered and you pay for units used.

International calls are best made at a post office where you have a numbered booth, dial your number and pay at the counter after your call. During the summer months the lines are busy and lengthy delays can be expected. The dialling code for the UK us 00 - 44, then dial the subscribers code and number. In the case where the code starts with 0, this is omitted. For example, for London (081) just dial 81. It is cheaper to phone the UK between 2000 and 0800 hrs.

To telephone locally in the Algarve, you need to use the area code, but you do not use the code if you are telephoning within the area: 082 is the area code from Sagres to Guia (just west of Albufeira); 089 from Guia to Fuseta (just east of Olháo); 081 from Fuseta to Vila Real de Santo António.

Telegraph

Telegrams *(Telegrama)* may be sent from post offices in Faro, Lagos, Portimão, Tavira, Vila Real de Santo António, Albufeira, Vilamoura, Praia da Luz and from some hotel receptions.

Telex and fax
The Post Offices in Faro and Portimão have public telex facilities. Some hotels and travel agents will accept telex using their own telex number. The fax system has now been introduced and in a number of uses is taking over from telex.

Currency and banks

The Algarve is part of Portugal and therefore the currency is the escudo. One escudo, which is written 1 $ 00, comprises 100 centavos. There are notes for 5,000, 1,000, 500, 100 and 50 escudos, and coins for 50, 25, 20, 10, 5, 2.50, and 0.50 escudo. 1,000 escudos is called a conto. High priced items are often quoted in contos, a point to be observed when shopping.

There is no limit to the amount of foreign currency that can be brought into the Algarve, but at present no more than 50,000 escudos per person may be brought in. As a matter of interest you cannot obtain Spanish pesetas from any of the banks.

The 'high street' banks in the Algarve have names like Banco Espirito Santo, Banco Portuguese do Atlântico and Banco Borges. There is a branch of Lloyds Plc in Avenida 5 de Outubro, 33, Faro 8000. Tel: 089 83919/83951.

Most banks accept Eurocheques (with encashment cards) and international credit cards like Visa and Access. When you go to the bank you will need your passport. Banks are open from 0830 to 1145 and 1300 to 1445 hrs, Monday to Friday. The currency exchange rate is displayed in banks, travel agents and hotels, where you may also cash traveller's cheques and change currency. A small commission is charged for this service. International credit cards are generally accepted in hotels, restaurants and a number of shops.

Hotels usually have deposit boxes for guests to secure their valuables. The Portuguese in the Algarve are generally law abiding, but it is sensible to take precautions against pickpockets when in towns and country markets.

Electricity

Electricity is supplied at 220 volts, 50 cycles. You will require a two-pin plug or a continental adapter to use equipment such as a hair dryer.

Festivals and events

Throughout the year there are festivals and fairs in Portugal and the Algarve. The markets sell everything imaginable in the way of food, clothes, radios, animals, buckets, linen and pottery.

Festival time finds the streets decorated with flowers and coloured lights, likewise the churches and public buildings. There will be local bands playing and folk dancing. The Algarve Regional Tourist Board distributes a calendar of events to hotels and other accommodation. Some of these are:

February   The Almond Blossom International Cross Country Race. Some of the world's best athletes take part in this twelve-kilometre race. There are facilities for thousands of spectators.

February   Carnival Time: The week before Lent, held in various towns. Loulé is the centre of this activity in the streets, with processions and much revelry.

April/May   Portuguese Golf Open at the Quinto do Largo.

May/June   Musical Festival: A series of concerts, recitals and ballet.

June   Beer Festival: There are folk dancing groups, musicians and general dancing, also sampling of beer produced in Portugal and the Algarve.

September   National Folklore Festival: Folkdance groups from all areas dance and wear their regional dress.

November   The International Algarve Car Rally: Driving championship.

Fire precautions

Fire precautions are observed throughout the Algarve, with public buildings, including hotels, being inspected for adequate fire escape equipment. Fire emergency instructions should be displayed in your hotel or apartment block. Modern fire-fighting equipment is located in the major towns. The emergency telephone number to call the Fire Fighting Services (Bombeiros) is 115. They can also be contacted in Lagos on 082 62943; Portimão, 082 22122; Albufeira, 089 53333; Faro, 089 22122; and Tavira 081 22122.

Hairdressing

Men's barbers are called *barbeiros,* ladies and unisex salons *cabeleireiros.* A man's haircut costs 400 escudos (£1.60) to 1,000 escudos (£4), and a woman's cut and blow dry from 1000 escudos (£4) to 1,500 escudos (£6), shampoo and set from 900 escudos (£3.60) to 1,300 escudos (£5.20). The larger hotels have hairdressing salons where the staff understand English and have modern equipment, but it will probably cost more. Some ladies' hairdressers in the Algarve are:

Teresa Marina Shopping Centre, Vilamoura. Tel: 089 32386.

Hairway Rua Alves Correira 79, Albufeira. Tel: 089 52448.

Hair by Design Rua das Portas de Portugal, Lagos (opposite the Post Office).

Style In Above Ancona Bar, Areiras de San João. Tel: 089 55655.

Health

There are no dangerous animals or poisonous reptiles in the tourist resorts along the Algarve. In dry mountain areas you may encounter the only venomous snake, a viper. At times, when it is warm and has been raining, flies and mosquitos (especially at Monte Gordo) can be a nuisance. So take some anti-mosquito cream with you.

Although the Algarve faces the North Atlantic Ocean, the character of the climate is Mediterranean and a healthy one, with sea breezes moving the air on most days, even during summer when it gets quite hot (the most 75°F/24°C in July and August). In the winter it is never extremely cold (54°F/12°C in January) but will be cooler, of course, inland in the mountains.

Usually the greatest health problem to visitors is caused by over indulgence of different types of food and drink, and probably too much time spent lying in the hot sunshine. Care must be taken to ensure that salads and fruit are quite clean before being consumed. The tap water in the Algarve is quite safe to drink, but if there is any doubt in your mind about this bottled water can be purchased from bars and supermarkets; it is cheap and pleasant to drink. Aerated water is called *agua com gas,* still water is *agua sem gas.*

Cases of upset tummies or diarrhoea are not to be expected but should these occur avoid alcoholic drinks and salads. A chemist *(farmácia)* should be consulted to obtain a suitable medicant. These are open during normal business hours, and, as in the UK, a rota of those that are open at later hours is published. Your hotel reception should be able to advise you.

Be careful to avoid too much exposure of the body to the sun; beware especially of falling asleep whilst sun bathing. The sun's rays are very strong in the Algarve because of the low humidity and clear atmosphere. The wearing of sun glasses, hats and the early use of suntan lotion or cream is sensible. Do not wait until the skin is turning red. That may be too late. Sunstroke can be very distressing. Symptoms are a severe headache, vomiting and much physical discomfort. Mild cases require a cool, shaded room with plenty of liquid to drink (lemonade, *gasosa,* is helpful). Apply a calomine or similar cream to parts affected by the sun. If the skin is blistered or symptoms are not improving, do not hesitate to consult a health centre, doctor or chemist. Hotel receptions have addresses and telephone numbers.

Laundry and dry cleaning

All hotels operate a laundry service *(lavandarias)* and dry cleaning *(tinturarias)* can be arranged. A three-day service is usual, but it is possible to have it done in less time. It is advisable to ascertain that your garment will be returned before you leave the Algarve.

Examples of laundry costs: blouse 250 escudos (£1); shirt 250 escudos (£1); pyjamas 300 escudos (£1.20); nightgown 250 escudos (£1); trousers 350 escudos (£1.40).

Markets

Every town in the Algarve has a daily market, where in the morning you can buy fresh meat, fish, fruit and vegetables. These places are colourful and lively and even if you do not wish to make a purchase it is worth a visit to observe the Algarvíos at work in their natural surroundings. Be prepared at some of these markets to communicate by sign language as, of course, not all stall holders speak English. It is useful too, to have some small change as it is not helpful to proffer a large bank note. Outdoor markets, which are *tipico* and fun, are held weekly. The dates of these events can be had from your local tourist information office or hotel. The monthly *Algarve Magazine* also lists market dates. Some monthly markets are:

Albufeira Albufeira, First and third Tuesday; Pademe, First Saturday.

Alcoutim Vaqueiros, Second Thursday; Pereiro, Fourth Sunday.

Aljezur Rogil, Second Monday; Aljezur, Third Monday.

Castro Marim Azinhal, First Sunday, except May.

Faro Estoi, Second Sunday.

Lagos Lagos, First Sunday; Odeáxere, Fourth Monday; Bensafrim, Second Monday.

Loulé Loulé, Every Saturday; Alte, Third Thursday; Benafim, First Saturday; Ameixial, First Thursday; Boliqueime, Last Thursday; Quarteira, Every Wednesday; Salir, First Tuesday; Cortelha, First Saturday; Montes Novos, Third Sunday; Almancil, Second and fourth Thursday.

Monchique Monchique, Second Friday.

Olhao Moncarapacho, First Sunday; Fuseta, First Thursday.

Portimão Portimão, First Monday.

S. Brás de Alportel , Every Saturday.

Silves Silves, Third Monday; Algos, Second Monday; S. Bartolomeu de Messines, Fourth Monday; S. Marcos da Serra, First Monday; Armação de Pera (April and May) First Sunday, (June to September) First and Third Sunday, (October to March) First Thursday.

Tavira Tavira, Third Monday; Cabeça Gorda, First Saturday; Santa Catarina, Fourth Sunday; Alcaria do Cume, Second Saturday; Portela da Corcha, Fourth Saturday.

Vila do Bispo Sagres, Every Friday.

Vila Real de Santo António Vila Nova de Cacela, Third Sunday.

Medical services

It is advisable to take out personal medical insurance when travelling abroad. This can be arranged through your travel agent, tour operator or insurance company. In addition, British visitors should be in possession of a Form E111 when visiting the Algarve (Portugal belongs to the European Community), obtainable from your local Department of Health and Social Security. This will enable you to receive emergency medical treatment whilst in the Algarve, under a bilateral agreement between Portugal and the UK. Without this, or personal medical insurance, treatment can be expensive.

Doctors

There are English-speaking medical practitioners in the Algarve and well equipped general hospitals, as well as good private clinics. For a visit to a doctor or for a consultation the cost would be about 1,500 escudos (£6) and the payment is required at the time of the visit, with further costs for subsequent treatments. It is advisable to set aside some escudos, in case you should need them in an emergency at a time when the banks are closed or it is difficult to change money. Do not forget to ask the doctor for a receipt of payment for the purpose of your insurance claim; they are used to supplying these. Tourist offices and hotels have addresses and telephone numbers of doctors, but in an emergency telephone 115.

The general hospitals in Faro (tel: 089 22011) and Portimão (tel: 082 22132) have a 24-hour service. There are hospitals in Lagos (tel: 082 63034), Monchique (tel: 082 92413), Silves (tel: 082 42416), Lagoa (tel: 082 52102), Albufeira (tel: 089 52133), Tavira (tel: 081 22133), Vila Real de Santo António (tel: 081 43116). Many towns have 14-hour private clinics.

Dentists

Dentists are fully qualified, their service is good and they use modern equipment. Generally, as a tourist you can call at the surgery and take your turn. Either the dentist or his receptionist will speak English. Be sure that your holiday insurance policy covers you for emergency dental treatment. As with doctors, dental treatment has to be paid for as received. A receipt for your insurance claim will be supplied on request.

There is an English dental surgeon at Almancil (Vivenda Gil 2 A-B, Rua do Vale Formoso. Tel: 089 95453), which is about ten kilometres west of Faro on the main EN125 road to Albufeira. The surgery is 500m from the traffic lights on the road to Loulé. In tourist areas the hotel reception or your tour representative will know where to find the nearest dentist.

Opticians

Opticians provide a reliable service. In the larger towns like Faro, Albufeira, Portimão and Lagos, they are able to test your vision and supply spectacles at short notice. In some cases you can claim on your insurance for broken or lost lenses, therefore a receipt needs to be obtained for work carried out.

Newspapers and books

English daily and Sunday newspapers can be obtained at the airport, major towns, tourist resorts and the larger hotels, usually the day after publication. The cost is about double that in the UK. Some English and American periodicals and comics are available. There is a large selection of English paperbacks to be bought in bookshops *(a livraria)* if you are prepared to pay the higher price.

The Algarve has its own newspaper in English, The *Algarve News,* published fortnightly on a Friday and costing 50 escudos (£0.20). It is a very useful newspaper and visitors are advised to obtain a copy on arrival. It contains 32 pages of news about the Algarve as well as some national and international news. There are many advertisements, letters, recipes and a "what's on" section covering fairs, markets, sport, art, cinemas, TV programmes, and church services, as well as information about buses and taxis. There are also 34-page newspapers covering the regions which are free from hotels and Tourist Information Offices, *Discover Eastern Algarve, Discover Faro, Discover Vilamoura, Discover Portimao* and *Discover Lagos* are published monthly and contain a great deal of information about bars, restaurants, services, shops, entertainments, recreation and property.

In addition, there is the glossy *Algarve Magazine* with colour pictures published monthly and costing 400 escudos (£1.60). It is also on sale in the UK. Its contents are topical and range from art, books, and personalities to descriptions of places of interest.

Police

The police wear dark blue uniforms in towns and are responsible for traffic control there, and for maintaining public order. Some wear red arm bands marked CD. This means that they can speak foreign languages and are available to assist tourists. In rural areas the police wear brown uniforms. There are women police. All police are generally helpful and are quite numerous in towns.

There are white police cars and police motor cycles on the highways. They make speed checks and examine documents.

To call for police assistance telephone 115. This emergency number can also be used to call an ambulance or the fire service.

The graceful Praça do Marquis do Pombal is a peaceful spot to have some refreshment, enhanced by the fragrant blossom of orange trees, that line the town square of Vila Real de Santo António.

Problems and complaints

The best place to go if you have a complaint about your accommodation is a tourist office. The head office is in the Rua da Misericórdia, Faro. Tel: 089 25404 or 24067. Other offices are located at Albufeira, Armação de Pera, Lagos, Portimão, Praia da Rocha, Silves, Tavira, Vila Real de Santo António, Olhâo, Quarteira, Carvoeiro and Loulé. But usually the hotel reception, or tour operator representative would rather sort out any problem you may have. In extreme cases of distress it may be necessary to go to the police (see Police) or British Consul (see British Consul).

Public conveniences

Public conveniences, as found in the UK, hardly exist in the Algarve and should not be relied on. Generally the public use the facilities provided by a bar, café, restaurant or hotel. It is not necessary to be a customer, but they prefer it when you are! Pictographs are often used to distinguish the 'Ladies' *(Senhora)* and the 'Gentlemen' *(Cavalheiro)* — a shoe, hat or figure on the door.

Public holidays

During the year there are quite a number of events taking place in the Algarve, so you may like to time your visit here to attend some occasion of interest to you. The exact dates of some of these celebrations can change, but the Portuguese National Tourist Office (1-5 Bond Street, London W1Y 0NP. Tel: 071 493 3873) should be able to help you by providing an up-to-date calendar of events.

Remember that on public holidays, shops, offices and banks will be closed. A few shops may be open in tourist resorts and certainly most cafés, bars and restaurants. Bus and train services are likely to be curtailed and petrol filling stations closed. Information will be provided by the tourist office of the area where you are staying and probably the hotel reception or tour operator representative.

National holidays are as follows (shops, offices and banks may also close on 24 and 26 December):

1 January	— New Year's Day
Movable	— Shrove Tuesday

Movable	— Good Friday
25 April	— Anniversary of the 1974 Revolution
1 May	— Labour Day
10 June	— Portuguese National Day
Movable	— Corpus Christi
15 August	— The Assumption
5 October	— Anniversary of the First Republic
1 November	— All Saints' Day
1 December	— Restoration
8 December	— The Immaculate Conception
25 December	— Christmas Day

Radio

News, weather, sport and music are broadcast by Radio Lagoa, FM 99.4 mhz. There are programmes in English, Monday to Saturday from 1800 to 2000 hrs and on Sunday from 1800 to 1830 hrs. Radio Algarve, FM 100.7, 101.6 and 101.9 mhz, broadcasts a programme in English from 0900 to 1000 hrs.

Shopping

Shopping in the Algarve is very much the same as in the UK and Europe, though shopping hours are from 0900 to 1300 and 1500 to 1900 hrs. On Saturday shops close at 1300 hrs, and close all day Sunday, except in the tourist resorts where supermarkets and souvenir shops may be open in the morning. The ubiquitous supermarkets are found in every town, village and tourist complex. These days most hotels and apartment blocks include their own supermarket, where all goods are price marked. The weight is by kilogramme (2.2lb) or part thereof; measurement is by metre (see Appendix C for conversion tables).

Shopping baskets are available in some of the larger stores. Any personal parcels may have to be deposited at the entrance where a numbered tag is given as a receipt. In tourist areas the shop assistants will understand English and generally are pleasant and helpful. In some shops you are expected to select your own vegetables, but in others an assistant will serve you. At the delicatessen, meat, fish and cheese counter you will be served. It may be necessary to take a numbered ticket to get your place in the queue for service. A good selection of frozen food is to be found: local fish and meat are prepacked and frozen at a reasonable price.

In Faro, Lagos, Portimão and Vila Real de Santo António the old quarters have been closed to traffic and made into pedestrian shopping areas. Here you can browse at leisure amongst boutiques, art galleries, bookshops and cafés as well as the usual shops. In the small villages shopping will be slower with time allowed for gossiping. Even now there are no large department stores to be found but high fashion clothes and modern household goods are plentiful.

The quality and smartness of Portuguese clothing makes shopping for a bargain quite a possibility. Shoes especially can be of a high standard of workmanship. It is a good idea to know your continental size (see Appendix C).

The old Algarvios women have the skill and patience to make beautiful lace mats, but it is a time-consuming art.

Souvenirs

The Algarve is a good place to shop for souvenirs that range from high class art work and porcelain to simple jewellery and sea shells. Few items are actually made in the Algarve, except for some of the hand-knitted woollen garments, basketwork and ceramics. However, Portugal produces a large selection of useful items.

Azulejos These are hand painted glazed tiles of different colours, sizes and motifs. For many years they have been used to decorate churches and stately homes. Nowadays every Algarvian household has them on their patio walls, tables and kitchens. You can buy a single tile or set specially packed for export.

The Barcelos cockerel

A pilgrim on his way to Santiago de Compostela (so the story goes) was accused of theft as he was about to leave Barcelos. In spite of pleading his innocence, he was condemned to death by hanging. The judge refused to listen to his pleas, until the pilgrim noticed the judge's repast of roast cockerel and declared that, to prove his innocence, the cock would stand up and crow. The miracle happened and the prisoner was freed. In memory of the occasion the pilgrim erected a monument of the cockerel, which may now be seen in the archaeological museum in Barcelos.

Today, this highly colourful red rooster is a Portuguese National emblem and copies of the statue, in a wide variety of sizes, are on sale in tourist shops all over Portugal and the Algarve.

Ceramics Highly decorated pieces of pottery come in all shapes and sizes, from huge vases to tiny eggcups. Prices vary so it is worthwhile looking around, and do check the quality of the glazing. Dark brown earthenware pottery, often in kitchenware, is reasonable and useful. A true souvenir is to buy a ceramic 'Red Rooster', the national emblem of Portugal.

Copper Candlesticks, bowls and trays are easy to pack and make a lasting gift. There is some pewter, too. You can see the craftsmen at work in Loule.

Cork Portugal has many cork trees whose bark is converted into place mats and unusual ornaments.

Cottons You will find a range of cotton goods at competitive prices include teeshirts, trousers, bedspreads and cotton rugs.

Dolls There are dolls of all sizes in authentic Algarvian costume and from the different regions of Portugal.

Embroidery Handmade tablecloths, mats and shawls from Madeira make popular souvenirs. You will have to search hard for locally-made lace items.

Jewellery Delicate filigree necklaces, earrings and bracelets are costly but easy to pack. There is plenty of modern jewellery in gold and silver and less expensive materials.

Leather Look for shoes, belts and jackets.

Liqueurs and wine From almonds comes a liqueur called Algarviana, which has a slightly bitter flavour. The Lagoa wine comes from the Algarve. Most unusual is Medronho, made from the small strawberry-like berry of the arbutus tree.

The strawberry like fruits of the medronheiro tree.

Marble Local marble is heavy to transport, but is made into attractive ornaments, candlesticks and vases.

Sweets In this area you'll find lots of nice things to tempt you, from sugared almonds to marzipan fruits and animals.

Woollens Both machine and hand-knit woollen garments are an excellent buy: fishermen's pullovers, cardigans and jumpers in all sizes and colours.

Wicker Some is made locally, some is imported from Madeira. You'll find a large selection of well made items, trays, baskets and potholders. There are also Chinese-made goods.

Television

Television programmes are received by satellite in the Algarve. To receive these you require a satellite dish receiver. Some hotels have TV cables into rooms and many of the programmes are in English. A TV guide appears in the English newspaper *Algarve News*, published fortnightly and costing 50 escudos (£0.20). Video cassettes are now as popular in the Algarve as elsewhere in Europe.

Time

Time is the same in the Algarve, Portugal and the UK. The clocks change by one hour for summer and winter, at the end of March (forward) and October (back).

Tipping

Tipping is expected as in the UK and on the Continent. In bars, cafés and restaurants (except where a service charge may have been added to the bill) a tip in the region of ten per cent may be given, perhaps less for a drink at the bar. Maids and porters handling luggage should be tipped. Taxi drivers expect a ten per cent tip, but generally the *Algarvíos* are well mannered and do not make much of the subject.

SEVEN

Food and drink

The Algarve offers a great variety of food from all over the world, to cater for the large number of international tourists visiting the region. With new modern restaurants opening in the luxury developments, there are eating places to suit all tastes. The local inhabitants now join with their visitors in enjoying exotic dishes.

Prices in the Algarve for fresh produce are reasonable, but imported foods tend to be priced a little higher than in the UK and the rest of Europe.

Foods on the menu

Many of the fruits and vegetables you will choose from are grown in the Algarve. Delicious strawberries *(morangos)*, peaches *(pêssagos)*, melons *(melâos)*, figs *(figos)* and grapes *(uvas)* are delivered fresh to many eating establishments. The selection of vegetables includes potatoes *(batatas)*, onions *(cebolas)*, cabbage *(couve)*, cauliflower *(couveflor)*, beans *(feifao)*, cucumber *(pepino)*, parsley *(salsa)*, spinach *(espinafres)* and mushrooms *(cogumelos)*. Rice *(arroz)* is usually available. Locally cured hams *(fiambres)*, much fresh fish *(peixe)*, and of course eggs *(ovos)* and cheeses *(queijos)* are ordered daily by restaurants, cafés and hotels.

The staple diet of the Algarvíos is fish, with cod *(bacalhau)* being the most popular and versatile: it is eaten boiled, baked, fried and, best of all, as a stew. The Portuguese are fond of boiled fish served with cabbage, boiled potatoes and seasoned with oil and vinegar.

Shell fish *(mariscos)* is also popular. Prawns *(gambas)*, crabs *(caranguejos)*, lobsters *(langostas)*, mussels *(mexilhões)*, octopus *(polvo)*, cockles *(ameijoas)* and tunny fish *(atum)* all form part of many Portuguese menus. A real treat is to eat fresh grilled sardines *(sardinhas grelhadas)*.

Chicken *(frango)* and rabbit *(coelho)* are always on country menus. Pork *(porco)* and suckling pig *(leitão)* are often barbecued. You will also find other meat *(carne):* beef *(vaca),* steak *(bife)* and rumpsteak *(entrecosta).*

Some useful words to know when selecting from a menu are: assado (roasted), cozido (boiled), estufado (stewed), *no forno* (baked), *no espeto* (on the spit), *frito* (fried), *bem passado* (well done), *mal passado* (rare) and *medio* (medium).

A green or mixed salad *(saladas)* is seldom served with meals, unless ordered as a first course. If you feel like an appetiser, look on the menu under *(petiscos).* Other starters may be melon with ham *(melão com presunto)* or snails flavoured with oregano *(caracoise a Algarvia).*

Some local dishes

Soups

Caldo verde Thick potato and cabbage soup *(sopa)* with smoked sausage.

Sopa de coziao A meat soup with vegetables and macaroni.

Gaspacho A chilled soup made from diced sweet peppers, onions, cucumber, tomatoes and served with croutons.

Fish

Bacalhau à Brás Dried cod fried with onions and potatoes, cooked in beaten egg.

Caldeirada Several kinds of fish simmered with onions, tomatoes, potatoes and olive oil. Excellent.

Panada A stew made with mussels, cockles, onions, garlic and coriander. Eggs are cracked into it to poach, just before serving.

Ameijoas cataplana Clams, sausage, ham, onion, garlic, paprika, chili sauce, parsley and white wine, cooked in a *cataplana* — an oval dish made of metal with a lid, in which all ingredients cook in their own juices. After cooking on a gas stove the *cataplana* dish is turned upside down for a few minutes before being served at table.

Meat

Bife no frigideira Beef steak fried in butter, white wine and garlic, served with ham and fried bread.

Cozido à Portugesa Boiled beef, bacon, sausage and vegetables, served with rice.

Enjoyed by Algarvios and tourists alike, tasty charcoal grilled sardines, are a succulent meal.

Cabrito estufado Casserole of young goat, with potatoes, onions, tomatoes and peas.

Carne de parco comameijoas Chunks of pork cooked on a spit with clams, tomatoes and onions.

Espetada mista Kebab of beef, lamb and pork.

Farnago de churrasco Barbecued chicken with a spicy pimento sauce called 'piri piri'.

Desserts

The local puddings are all very sweet, often made with almonds, figs and eggs.

Farofias Beaten egg white, poached in milk, topped with cinnamon and honey.

Fios de ovos Fine strands of egg yolk cooked in syrup.

Pudim Molotov Egg white mousse in caramel sauce.

Pudim flan Caramel custard.

You may be offered fruits *(frutas)* such as apple *(maca)* apricot *alperces)*, banana *(banana)*, orange *(laranja)*, pear *(pera)*, nuts *(avelas)*.

Cheese

Portuguese cheeses are usually a mixture of sheep and goat's milk or cow and goat's milk. *Cabreiro* is a fresh goat's milk cheese. *Serra da estrela* is ewe's milk cheese and very rich.

Cakes and biscuits

Bolo podre A cake flavoured with honey and cinnamon.

Bolo de arroz Rice cake.

Boas de mel Little honey-flavoured biscuits.

Massapaes Almond macaroons.

Queijada A small cottage cheese tart.

Tarte de almendoa Almond tart.

Bolo de chila do Algarve Biscuits of pumpkin jam, grated almonds, egg yolks and sugar. If you like sticky sweetness, have a *pastel de tenugal,* which is very thin flaky pastry filled with a beaten egg yolk mixture and cooked in syrup.

Drinks

Tea is drunk in the Algarve, both by the inhabitants and tourists. It is served black with either milk *(leite)* or lemon *(limoa)*. If you require more hot water ask for *aqua quente*. Afternoon tea is

This peaceful scene is at Vila Real in the spring sunshine.

popular in many tourist areas and can be a meeting and social occasion. Sometimes a musician will entertain customers, like the organist in the beach cafeteria of the Hotel Sol E Mar, Albufeira. In Vilamoura the Cakes and Tea Rooms serve delicious almond pie and mixed fruit cakes with a good selection of teas. It is open from 0830 to 0030 hrs.

Coffee *(cafe)* is served everywhere. A small cup of black espresso coffee is a *bica;* with a few drops of milk it is a *garoto;* white coffee served in a tall glass is called a *galao.* Sugar *(acucar)* is optional. You can also order a glass of milk *(um copo de leite).*

Water *(agua)* can be bought in supermarkets and hotels as well as cafés, bars and restaurants. Mineral water *(agua mineral)* can be aerated *(com gas)* or still *(sem gas).*

Non alcoholic drinks *(bebidas nao alcoolicas)* are lemon juice *(uma limonada)* orangeade *(uma laranjada),* orange juice *(um sumo de lananja),* and tonic water *uma agua tonica.* Look for bars advertising juices *(sucos)* and you can try papaya *(mamao),* mango *(manga),* pineapple *(abacaxi),* and sugar cane juice *(caldo de cana).*

Beer *(cerveja)* is a drink much enjoyed in the Algarve and the variety of imported brands is large. Some, like Carlsberg, are bottled here under licence. Local beers such as Sagres can be light or dark; they are served chilled bottled or from a barrel. A small draught beer is *uma imperial,* a lager is *uma cerveja.*

Portuguese wines and spirits

Portugal has many worthy wines which are available in the Algarve at reasonable prices. The Vinhos Verdes, served chilled, can be red or white and are made from under-ripe grapes and have a slightly lower alcohol content. There are stronger wines from the Duro Valley. Sparkling wines like Vino Espumante, Raposeira and Mateus Rosé are popular. A light and sweet wine is the Moscatel from Setúbal. Should you wish for the house wine *(vinho da casa),* ask for red *(tinto)* or white *(branco).*

(Opposite) *The fishermen's beach at Albufeira, with attractive white cottages, colourful boats, warm seas and golden sands, typifies the coastal attraction of the Algarve.*

Maybe you will prefer to keep to Portugal's most famous drink. In 1678, two Englishmen were puzzling about how to ship a large consignment of wine back to Britain and keep it in good condition. They decided to add a little brandy to each cask, and thus the great port wine was created.

The Algarve has its own wines, Algar Seco from the Lagoa region, red, white and rosé, about 13.5°, and Alfonso 111, rather like a sherry and better served chilled. The other wine from the Algarve is from the Tavira region and is 12.5°, a pleasant drink found in most supermarkets.

Portuguese brandy *(Conhaque* or *Aguardente velhe)* has a distinctive flavour; try Borges or Constantino. If you really want fire water *Baghaco* is the local stuff. *Ginjinha* is another fiery drink made from morello cherries. You have been warned! To end on a sweet note, *Brandymel* is a honey-based liqueur.

Bars and cafés

Along the south coast every town and village has an abundance of bars and cafés. In the country villages these are not always obvious to the passerby, the entrance can be behind a net curtain. In the newer tourist complexes, bars and cafés with eyecatching names compete for tourist custom. Shots in the Dark, in Lagos, is open from 1500 to 0200 hrs daily, with a long 'happy hour' when two drinks are for the price of one. The Sleeping Donkey in Olhos d'Agua, Albufeira, is near the beach where John and Carol are usually around for a chat. Here you can have an English breakfast until noon and snacks all day. The Kingfisher Inn in Olhão is where yachtsmen like to congregate, it is English owned and closed on Tuesdays. Mac's Bar on the Tavira/São Bras De Alportel road is open from 1130 hrs and advertises 'Sassenachs Welcome'. You can get a good Ploughman's Lunch here too.

Snack bars are open from 0800 hrs and only close when the last customer leaves after midnight. Often the disco music from one bar merges with the sound of jazz next door. Many bars and cafés have tables outside. usually service is fast and cheerful and customers are never pressured to leave.

(Opposite) *A visit to the old town of Loulé can include seeing craftsmen at work, busy making decorated saddles, harnesses and bridles. A skill reputed to have been handed from the time of the Moors.*

Restaurants

The choice of restaurants in the Algarve is vast and as good as anywhere along the Mediterranean coast. There are, for instance, 31 in the Vilamoura complex alone.

Restaurants are government inspected and rated according to a scale of four classes — luxury *(de luxo)*, first, second and third class. However, the rating does not necessarily relate to the quality of the food, but the higher the class the higher the charge. A sign denoting the class is usually shown outside the restaurant with the menu prices, which may also include tax and service charge. If no service charge is included a tip for good service in the region of 5 or 10 per cent should be given.

Meal times vary but in restaurants breakfast *(o pequeno almoço)* is served until 1000 hrs, lunch *(o almoço)* is from noon until 1500 hrs and dinner *(o jantar)* from 1930 to 2130 hrs (earlier than in Spain). Most restaurants have an international menu that includes Portuguese dishes, however some do specialise. You will find Brazilian, English, Chinese, German, Indonesian, Italian and Indian restaurants as well as pizza houses and health food establishments. Your hotel reception, tour operator representative or the local newspaper will help you decide where to eat. It's also a good idea to ask fellow guests in your hotel.

The authors would like to emphasise that in the popular tourist resorts a number of restaurants and cafés change owners and chefs, so standards can vary from season to season. All those listed here have been graded by the Portuguese National Tourist Office. As with the selection of hotels, these restaurants and cafés are listed in order of towns going from east to west of the Algarve.

Vila Real de Santo António

Caves do Guadiana (class 2) Avenida da Republica 89, Tel: 44498. On the seafront. Seafood, giant prawns and Portuguese dishes.

Dom Jotta (class 2) Ponta de Santo António, Tel: 43151. Typical Portuguese bar/restaurant, by sea and river.

O Fantastico (class 3) Avenida Professor Egas Moniz, Tel: 43692. In a back street, near the bullring and fire station. Fresh fish, Portuguese food, *tipico*. Recommended for local atmosphere.

Nova Grelha (class 2) Rua Dr Manuael de Arriaga. Tel: 42720. Large restaurant close to shopping precinct, good for grills. Families welcome.

Monte Gorde

Alcazar Coffee Shop (class 3) Rua de Ceuta, Tel: 42184. Part of Hotel Alacazar. Snack bar, restaurant; pleasant and good value. Recommended.

O Patio (class 3) Avenida Infante D Henrique, Tel: 44779. On the seafront. Above average decor. International and Portuguese cuisine. Recommended.

Pizeria Italia (class 3) Rua Tristao Vaz Teixeira, Tel: 42865. Quick service and clean. Pasta dishes.

Copacabana (class 2) Avenida Infante D Henrique, Tel: 42464. On the seafront with large patio. Snacks and international menu. Won a Gold Award 1988.

Tavira

America (class 3) Rua José Pires Padinha 2, Tel: 23330. Easy to locate by public gardens. Plain decor, good food, especially *cataplana* and seafood. Inexpensive.

Casa dos Frangos (class 3) Rua Jacques Pessoa 11, Tel: 22259. Simple restaurant. Good fresh fish and barbecued chicken.

English Rose (class 3) Rua Dr Mateus de Azevedo, Tel: 22247. Right in town centre, near post office. Spare ribs, home made burgers. Open 1200 to 1500 and 1800 hrs to midnight. Closed Sunday.

Imperial (class 3) Rua José Padinha. Chicken *à la maison* and *arroz de mariscos* are specialities.

Faro

Brasilia (class 3) Rua D Francisco Gomes 3. In the pedestrian precinct. Busy at lunch time. Seafood specialities. Unpretentious and inexpensive.

Cidade Velha (class 2) Rua Domingos Guiero 19, Tel: 27145. In the heart of the old walled city, near the cathedral. Established restaurant, international and Portuguese menu. Try fillet of pork stuffed with dates and walnuts. Open Monday to Friday 1230 to 1400 hrs and 1930 to 2230 hrs. Saturday 1930 to 2230 hrs. Reservations advised.

Dois Irmaos (class 3) Largo Terneiro de Bispo. Opened in 1925, this large restaurant has upstairs dining room with open fire in winter. Genuine Portuguese cooking.

Kappa (class 2) Rua Brites de Almeida 45, Tel: 23366. High class restaurant in city centre. Regional dishes include partridge, hare and pheasant in season.

Lady Susan (class 2) Rua 1 Dezembro. Tel: 28857. Gourmet fish dishes and light meals at bar. Closed at weekends.

La Pizza (class 3) Rua D Francisco Gomes. Clean, inexpensive quick service. On right side of precinct from seafront. Busy at lunchtime. Recommended.

O Gargalo (Class 3) Largo de Pe da Cruz, Tel: 27305. In good weather you can eat outside. Specialities *cataplanas* and seafoods. Credit cards accepted.

Sousa (class 3) Largo de Pe da Cruz, Tel: 26725. Near to central carpark, in attractive square. Blue tile decor, fast service. Good selection of fish dishes including grilled eels.

Vale do Lobo

Clube de Golf Tel: 94444. Daily lunch and dinner menu. Barbecue on Tuesday. Terrace view over golf course.

Casa da Torre Eritage Tel: 94329. One of the Algarve's top restaurants. Swiss operated. Dining terrace outside. French and Swiss menu. Pleasant ambience. Reservations required.

Tino's Tel: 94656. Near supermarket. International cuisine with French specialities. Flambées. Shell fish by order. Reservations required.

Quinta do Largo

Shepherds (de luxe) Tel: 94541. The restaurant with the upmarket name and style. Open Tuesday to Saturday. Portuguese specialities and international cuisine. Fine wines. Next door to Quinta do Largo Country Club. Reservations required.

Quarteira

Atlantico (class 3) Avenida Infante de Sagres, Tel: 35142. Located on promenade, overlooking the sea. Speciality barbecued chicken and fresh fish.

Belo Horizonte (class 2) Largo das Cortes Reais, Tel: 33739. Next to fish market. Air-conditioned, clean and well appointed. Speciality fresh fish and seafood.

Chinatown (class 3) Rua Vasco da Gama, Tel: 35408. Large menu of good Chinese food. Cosy atmosphere.

Michael's Kitchen (class 3) Rua Vasco da Gama, Tel: 32747. Small restaurant specialising in international and regional dishes. Good selection of desserts.

O Elegant (class 2) Old, established Portuguese restaurant near seafront at eastern end of town. Excellent choice of sea foods and local dishes. Reservations advised.

Vilamoura
Mayflower (class 3) Centro Comercial da Marina. Tel: 34690. Large, busy establishment near yacht marina. Seafood and international menu. Bar open 0900 hrs to midnight. Restaurant 1230 to 2330 hrs.

Albufeira
Alfredo Grill (class 2) Rua 5 de Outubro. Well established, small and pleasant. Inexpensive international menu. Recommended.
Ancora (class 2) Areias de Sáo João, Tel: 52665. Well estabished and busy with tourists. International menu, friendly service and good value. Serves breakfast, lunch and dinner. Open 0900 to 0200 hrs. Recommended.
A Ruina (class 3) Cais Herculano, Tel: 52094. On the seafront. Typical Portuguese, popular eating place with international menu.
Bombay Palace Areiras de Sán João, near Captain's Bar. Authentic Vindaloo and Tandori dishes. Owners also have Indian restaurant in London. Open from 1200 to 1500 hrs and 1800 to 2330 hrs, but closed on Monday.
Casa do Cerro (class 3) Cerro da Piedade, Tel: 52085. Typical Portuguese, with outside terrace. Grills, seafood and *arroz de tambril,* a speciality. Sunday night is *fado* entertainment. Open from 1200 to midnight.
O Cordovado Rua Alves Correia 44, Tel: 52146. Brazilian chef, menu, and waitresses. Extensive menu and live music.
Chor (class 2) Estrada Montechoro, Tel: 55727. You can dine in, or outside on the garden terrace. Specialities shell fish and *cataplana.* Open from 1830 to 2330 hrs.
Jade (class 2) Areias de Sán João, Tel: 52841. Chinese dishes Cantonese style. Lunch and dinner fixed price menu, also takeaway.
Mumtaz, Estrada do Montechoro. Indian menu includes Bhuna, Madras, Pasandra, Karai curries, also à la carte and children's menu.

Armação de Pera
Jardim (class 3) Rua General Humberto Delgardo, Tel: 33677. Well established, pleasant decor and terrace. Fish is the speciality, *cataplana, piri piri* prawns. English, French and German spoken. Closed Tuesday.
Lota (class 2) Rua da Praia, Tel: 33503. Steaks, kebabs, fish dishes and Portuguese menu. Breakfast 1030 to 1130, lunch 1230 and dinners. Closed Monday.

Silves
Dom Sancho (class 2) Largo do Castelo, Tel: 442437. Useful bar restaurant by the entrance to the castle. Notes for *piri piri,* spiced chicken. Souvenir shop.

Carvoeiro
A Rede (class 3) Estrada do Farol, Tel: 082 58513. Lovely patio for warm evenings. Good choice of seafood and meat dishes.

Portimão
A Lanterna (class 3) Near to bridge. Tel. 23948. Portuguese, fish soup, smoked swordfish and duck. Reasonable prices. Recommended.
Iemanja (Class 3) Rua Serpa Pinto 9. Tel: 23233. Decor is like a cave. The owners are fish dealers so fish is the speciality and you can choose from the window display.
Mariner's Pub (class 3) Rua Santa Isabel 28, Tel: 25848. To the north of town. Eighteenth century restaurant with lovely pub bar and live entertainment.
Mister Bojangles (class 3) Rua da Hortinha, Tel: 23042. Specialists in *fondue,* cooked at the table.
The Old Tavern (class 3) Rua Judice Fialho, Tel: 23325. At eastern end of town. Moorish arches and Crusader picture tiles. English run, international cuisine and seafood. Reservations advisable.

Lagos
Cacarola (class 2) Praça Luis de Camoes, Tel: 63883. Long established snack bar. Portuguese cooking, varied menu. Tables outside.
Cardapio (class 3) Rua 25 Abril 79, Tel: 61330. In centre of town. Portuguese owner. Charcoal grill and regional dishes at reasonable prices.
Dom Sebastiao (class 2) Rua 25 Abril, Tel: 62795. In centre of town. Portuguese owned, charcoal grill and regional dishes. Live shellfish and mature wines.
Jotta 13 (class 2) Rua 25 Abril, Tel: 62319. Well established and easily located in town centre. Charcoal grill, fresh sea food, good swordfish. Tourist menu 780 escudos (£3.12).
Lord's Tavern (class 3) Rua Antonio Crisogno dos Santos, Tel: 60296. Well known restaurant near Hotel Lagos, with good service and loud disco music.

Monchique Grill Penina Golf Hotel, Penina, Tel: 22051. Elegant candlelit atmosphere and attentive service. International menu on open charcoal grill, delicious chateaubriand. Well recommended for a special occasion dinner.

O Galeao (class 2) Rua da Lananjeira. Tel: 63909. Very good regional and international cuisine, almost in town centre. Portuguese and Swiss trained chefs. Reservations advised.

Taverna do Infante (class 3) Rua Marreiros Neto 50, Tel: 082 60327. Large, spacious bar restaurant. English breakfasts. Pub grub and music. Open 1000 to 1400 hrs and 1900 to 0200 hrs.

Sagres
Carlos (class 3) Esplanada. Clean and popular restaurant, so be prepared to wait. Excellent fresh fish, especially good swordfish. Reasonable house wines. Tables outside. Recommended.

The aroma of charcoal cooked chicken and spicy sausages greets tourists, as they look for souvenirs, close to the market in Silves.

The Penina golf course was the first championship course built in the Algarve. It is close to Lagos.

EIGHT

Leisure activities

Art galleries

The Algarve attracts many artists who are drawn to the region for its particular luminosity, colourful scenery, and the simple lifestyle of the countryfolk.

In the towns of Portimão and Lagos there are several well established art galleries. Newly opened in Vilamoura is **Galeria del Puerto,** Shop 4 by the Marina, which has an assortment of art works, antiques and craftwork. It is open from 1000 hrs to midnight. Also, quite recently opened in the mountain town of Monchique, is a cultural foundation called **Monchiqueiro,** which encourages young artists to exhibit their work. Tavira, too, has two separate art galleries in old buildings that have been restored — **Casa das Artes** and **Galeria de Arte** — where exhibitions of painting, sculpture and engraving are on show and for sale.

Perhaps the most interesting place of all is the **Centro Cultural,** São Lourenço, near Amancil. This is a delightful haven of culture and art, a private enterprise that is much praised by locals and visitors. It is a meeting place for young and old, with sculpture and art exhibitions of different nationalities, jazz concerts, classical music, conferences, films and social evenings all held in a picturesque old Portuguese house and attractive garden. It opens 1000 hrs until midnight. Do look out for the imaginative sculpture of the Portuguese sculptor, João Cutileiro, noted for his modern interpretation and simplicity of form.

Museums

Faro
The **Museu Etnografico Regional,** by the Jardim da Algoa, is a pleasant museum, where replica rooms of typical Algarve houses are furnished with authentic utensils, pottery, copper, iron, lace and

lifelike dummies in rustic costumes. There are also handicrafts, old photographs, fishing tackle, farm tools and chimneys.

In the old city is the **Museu Arqueológico e Lapidar Infante D. Henrique** (Prince Henry Archaeological and Lapidary Museum). This very interesting museum is well laid out in a former convent. Prehistoric and Roman archaeological treasures, large mosaics, busts, fossils, ceramics, furniture, paintings and stone coats of arms are some of the items on display.

Situated in the Harbourmasters building you will find the **Ramalho Ortigao Maritime Museu** (Maritime Museum). This small display shows items of navigation, model sailing boats, lanterns, paintings of fish and crustaceans, and fishing gear.

Lagos

The **Museu Regional de Lagos** is a splendid museum with unusual relics of folk and religious art: the original Charter of Lagos issued in 1504, Roman mosaics, saddles, rifles, objects in gold and silver, nineteenth-century surgical instruments. Set out in small rooms, each is a treasure trove relating to the region's past way of life and history. Closed on Monday.

Night life

The warm nights of the Algarve invite you to be out late at night because you find a happy carefree atmosphere wherever you stroll, whether on a moonlit beach, or amongst the cafés, bars and hotels. The tall palm trees and the sparkling seas under a starlit sky create a romantic setting. The choice is wide for your entertainment.

Nightclubs and discos

Next to the Montechoro Hotel, Albufeira, is **Michaels** where you can enjoy a three-course dinner, dancing and two floor shows every night, for 3,400 escudos (£13.60). The floor show includes glamorous show girls, magicians, clowns, singers and dancers. This is the place to take all the family and wear your glitter clothes.

Near the Bullring, Albufeira, is the **Crazy Bull e Magix** night club. This is a noisy fun place with UFO lighting and all the modern sounds. Open from 2200 to 0400 hrs is **Kiss, Albufeira**, one of the foremost nightclubs, with top DJs and plenty of music and entertainments for those that favour the bright lights.

The **Summertime Disco Club** in Montechoro has discos on two levels: at one level the mood is light and romantic while the other has the latest pop and disco dancing. It's open all week from 2200 to 0400 hrs. **Splash Disco Club,** Areis de S. João, is located in the Apartment Hotel Alfonso III, and is open 2230 to 1400 hrs. Most other tourist resorts have disco clubs.

Casinos

The Algarve has three casinos, at **Alvor, Monte Gordo** and **Vilamoura,** which open from 1700 until 0300 hrs. You are required to show your passport and gentlemen are requested to wear jackets. The games available are baccarat, blackjack, and roulette; there are slotmachines too. Entrance to the gaming rooms costs 1,100 escudos (£4.40). All the casinos have bars, restaurants and floorshows.

Cinemas

Some of the larger towns have cinemas with films from many countries, usually shown with the original dialogue and English sub-titles. At the **Black Bull complex** the S. João cinema has shows at 1600, 1830 and 2130 hrs, and sometimes at midnight. The cinema in the **Vilamoura complex** has shows at 1600 and 2130 hrs, with films in English.

There are also cinemas in **Lagos, Alvor, Portimao** and **Faro.**

Sports and pastimes

Archery

Archery can be practised at **Aldeia Dos Acoteias,** Albufeira, Tel: 089 66167. Here too are athletics and weight-lifting. There is also archery at the **Vila Real de Santo António Sports Pavilion, Tel: 081 44820.**

Bowling

There is a bowling green at the **Golden Beach Club,** Praia da Oura, Albufeira, Tel: 089 53135.

Bicycling

Bicycles can be hired at a number of places along the Algarve. Enquire at your hotel, tourist office or travel agent. Prices start from 500 escudos (£2) per day. This makes a pleasant way to travel as there are no steep hills along the coast roads.

Billiards

Billiards, snooker and pool tables are to be found in some bars, such as the **Bull Dog,** Albufeira, and in most of the large hotels.

Bird watching

Bird watching excursions are organised by the **West Algarve Riding Centre,** Lagos, Tel: 082 65152.

Bullfights

In Portugal bull fights differ from those in Spain, because the bull is not killed. Bull fights in the Algarve are advertised by posters and held in Vila Real de Santo António, Albufeira and Portimão. Usually they start promptly at 1700 hrs, but in summer, they may be delayed because of the heat until 2200 hrs.

Fishing

Some of the best sea fishing grounds are found in the Algarve at Sagres, Carrapateira, Monte dos Clérigos and Arrifana. The high season is from October to January. Scabbard fish, mullet, moray eel, bass, bream, tope and bluefish can be caught. Places where fishing expeditions are organised are **Praia da Luz, Alvor Praia** and **Vila Real de Santo Antonio.** A Big Game Fishing Centre, **Cepemar,** is at Vilamoura Marina, Tel: 089 33933.

Football

There are football stadiums at Faro, Lagos, Portimão and Vila Real de Santo António, where national and league games can be watched.

Golf

The Algarve is sometimes described as a 'golfer's paradise'. There are many courses, six of which are championship. These are:

Quinta do Largo Golf Club Faro, Tel: Amancil 94529. Built on the large, luxury estate of Quinto do Largo, this 27-hole championship course is flexible enough to play 17-hole combinations. Three 9-hole courses are, A - 2,870m; B - 2,950m; C - 2,895m. All par 36, SSS 72. The course was designed by the American, Bill Mitchell. Another 18-hole course is due to open in 1990. The Portuguese Open will be held here for three years, but the course can be enjoyed by all levels of golfers. Greens and fairways are kept fresh with sophisticated sprinklers controlled by a computer. Five wells and three reservoir lakes provide water for golf irrigation. There is an excellent practise ground, clubhouse, bar and restaurant.

Palmares Golf Club Lagos, Tel: Lagos 62961. Constructed on sandy soil, near Meia Praia, and designed by Frank Penninck, this 18-hole course has a 71 par, with three 5s, eleven 4s and four par 3s. It is situated within sight of sea and surrounding sand dunes and low pinewoods. Arrangements to play are by the day, week, fortnight or month. There are caddies, trolleys and golfcarts for hire. Golfers staying at the Hotel Lagos get free transport to the Palmares Golf Club.

Parque da Foresta Budens, Tel: 082 65333. Designed by José Pepe Gancedo, this course sixteen kilometres west of Lagos is 18 holes, 5,804m and par 72. Daily, weekly, fortnightly and monthly green fees can be arranged. Clubs, trolleys and golf buggies are for hire. There is a putting green and practice driving range, a new clubhouse with a pro shop and good locker rooms. The restaurant, bar and terrace overlook the course, with a sea view. A discount on fees is given to guests and owners of property at Parque da Foresta.

Penina Golf Club Portimão, Tel: Lagos 22051. Once a rice field, the longest and oldest of golf courses in the Algarve was built in 1966 and designed by Henry Cotton. A handicap certificate is required for the championship course. Medal tees, 6,263m, 18 holes par 73. Caddies, clubs, electric golf carts and trolleys are for hire and there is a practice driving range. Woods, water hazards and fifty foot trees, in beautiful quiet surroundings. Guests staying at the Penina Golf Hotel do not pay green fees.

Vale do Lobo Golf Club Almancil, Tel: Almancil 94444. Here there are three 9-hole courses: Yellow 3,036m par 36; Orange 2,975m par 36; Green 2,753m par 35. Clubs, golf carts and trolleys are for hire and there is a practice driving range. There's a clubhouse, pro shop, changing rooms and restaurant.

Vilamoura Golf Club Quarteira, Tel: 089 33652. It was designed by Trent Jones. The 18-hole championship course is 6,292m; the men's course is 5,886m; and the women's course is 5,244m. It is a fairly flat course with last part being through umbrella pine trees. A second 18-hole course has a championship length of 6,331m, par 73, SSS 72. The medal length is 5,955m (women's 5,149m). Caddies, clubs, trolleys and buggies are for hire. Lessons by professional are available all the year as well and there's a practice driving range. Facilities in the club house include bar, snacks and shop. The Vilamoura Golf Motel, with 52 rooms is next to the golf club. Tel: 089 32321.

(See also mini golf).

Horse riding

Plenty of riding stables are found in the Algarve. Many are along the coastline for riding on the sands. There are cross-country courses and jumping, and instruction is available. Some of these are the **West Algarve Centre,** Burgau, Tel: 082 65152; the **Paradise Riding Centre,** Almancil, Tel: 089 90166; **Riding Centre O Cangalho,** Barao de S. João, near Lagos, Tel: 082 67218; and the **Centro Hipico,** Mexilhoeiro Grande, a beautiful ranch in the foothills of Monchique, between Lagos and Portimão, Tel: 082 964443.

Microlights

For the intrepid aviator the **Algarve Microlight Centre** aerodrome is about one kilometre from Lagos, on the Portimão EN125 road. It is open daily from 0900 to 1200 and 1600 to 1800 hrs. Tel: 081 62906.

Mini golf

This is especially popular during the hot weather and there are courses at several hotels and clubs including the **Hotel da Aldeia,** Tel: 089 55031; the Vilamoura **Marinotel,** Tel: 089 33414; **Aldeia do Mar,** Tel: 089 35135; and the **Hotel Algarve,** Praia da Rocha, Tel: 089 2400.

Sailing

You can sail on the ocean or in the lagoons at Faro, Olhão, Portimão, Tavira, Vila Real de Santo António and the Vilamoura Marina. In these places you will find sailing dingies for hire, and some from hotels on the coast.

Shooting

Rough shooting for rabbit, partridge, hare, pigeon and quail can be arranged through the **Tavira Shooting Club.** There is a shooting club in the Vilamoura **Marinotel** (Tel: 089 33414); and the **Clube de Tiro** (gun club), which is set in its own grounds at the main entrance to Vilamoura, off the EN 125, and has many facilities, skeet shoots, automatic targets, Olympia trenches and hunting trails. Tel: 089 33133.

Skin diving, scuba and snorkelling

Where the beaches are rocky and there are cliffs, there is usually good diving. Near Carvoeiro at **Algar Seco** is a clear water lagoon that is a delight for snorkellers. For diving, try between Luz Bay and Sagres. Equipment for scuba diving is available for hire at the **Luz Bay Sea Sports Centre,** at Praia da Luz (Tel: 082 69538).

Sports centres

Sports centres in the Algarve provide a number of activities. The **Burgua Sports Centre** (Tel: 082 65350) is between Burgua and the main Lagos to Sagres road. Here you can swim and play squash, racquet ball, tennis and table tennis. There is also an aerobics health club, a multi gym and a sauna. Instruction is available. There is a restaurant and bar. Other sports centres are the **Vilamoura Health Club,** Tel: 089 33929; **Estalagem do Cerro,** Albufeira, Tel: 089 52191; **Monte Carvoeiro Fitness Club,** Tel: 082 57421; **Rock Garden Sports and Leisure Club,** Vilamoura, Tel: 089 34740 and the **Carveiro Clube de Tenis,** Tel: 082 57847.

Squash

Squash courts are to be found at the **Burgua Sports Centre** (Tel: 082 65350) (located between Burgua and the main Lagos to Sagres road); the **Carvoeiro Club** (Tel: 082 57266); **Hotel Alfamar,** Praia do Falesia (Tel: 089 66635); **Quinta da Balaia** (Tel: 089 55787); **Hotel Montechoro** (Tel: 089 52651); **Rotamar,** Altura (Tel: 081 95664); and the **Rock Garden Sport and Leisure Club,** Vilamoura (Tel: 089 34740).

Swimming

The sandy coast stretches for some ninety kilometres and faces south, so it is ideal for swimming. Use of beaches for swimming and water sports is free. There are numerous coves that invite naturists. On major beaches there are life guards in attendance and flags to indicate safety. A green flag indicates that it is safe to swim and a life guard is in attendance; yellow means caution, and a red flag means do not enter the water. (See also Chapter 1, Beaches).

Tennis

This sport is available everywhere on the Algarve, and there are many all weather courts that are also floodlit. The Carvoeira **Clube de Tenis** (Tel: 082 57847) has ten such courts, and there are some also at the **Hotel Montechoro,** Albufeira, Tel: 089 54021. The **Roger Taylor Tennis Centre,** Vale do Lobo (Tel: 089 94145) is one of Europe's top clubs with twelve courts, equipment and coaching available.

Walking

A good way of seeing the delightful countryside of the Algarve, is by walking. This can be done all the year round. The Tourist Office issues a free booklet *Guide to Walks* which lists some twenty walking routes, varying in distance from two to twelve kilometres, and describes the terrain. Even the experienced walker is advised to have this booklet.

Water ski-ing and windsurfing

These are popular sports. Equipment and instructors are available at the resorts and on lagoons east of Portimão. To name a few: **Hotel dos Navegadores,** Monte Gordo (Tel: 081 42490); **Hotel Vasco do Gama** (Tel: 081 44321); **Tavira Ski** (Tel: 081 22247); **Pedras D'el Rei,** Tavira (Tel: 081 22177).

NINE

The region and its people

History of the Algarve

Early colonisation

The name Algarve is thought to derive from the Arabic word *al-Gharb,* meaning 'west lands' or 'lands beyond', although the region is thought to have been inhabited long before the Moors arrived. One of the first occupants were probably the Cynetes (or a variant of that name), a primitive race from Andalusia. Later the coast was visited by Phoenicians, Celts and Carthaginians, who set up fishing colonies and traded in ivory and amber. The ancient Greeks also came to fish and mine copper.

However it was the Romans who established the first major settlements, arriving in 218 BC. They built roads, bridges and developed towns inland, constructing a successful irrigation system to support their colonies. Latin also forms a substantial component of the Portuguese language. The evidence of Roman occupation may still be seen throughout the Algarve today: at Milreu (near Estoi) lie the ruins of a Roman villa with mosaics and bathing pool, while the remains of a Roman settlement, Cerro da Vila, can be visited at a site near Vilamoura. At Castro Marim some of the walls of a Roman fortress bear witness to the scale of the Romans' colonisation. In those days Lagos was already a flourishing town known as Lacobriga, while near Portimão there are the remains of a salt tank used for preserving fish. The Romans are also said to have introduced Christianity to the region during the third century, establishing a Christian church at Faro.

The Moors arrive

With the fall of the Roman Empire some six centuries later the Algarve, like the rest of the Iberian peninsula, fell to the Vandals and later the Visigoths. Their influence remained unchallenged until the Moors rose to power in the eighth century. By 711 AD the Arabs had established a capital at Chelb, known today as Silves. Being a river port the city soon became the most important in the Algarve, with the influx of new wealth inspiring the construction of palaces and castles. Its strategic position was consolidated with fortified walls, behind which some 30,000 citizens enjoyed a cultured life amid bazaars and gardens.

Over the following centuries the Moorish influence spread through the region, their typical white cube houses and domed churches, still seen at Olháu, dotting the landscape. Prosperity came from fishing and rearing cattle. Some of the local Portuguese were converted to Islam, but the wars between Christian and Muslim continued all across Spain. Portuguese armies won and lost Faro several times before Count Alfonso Henriques, destined to become the first King of Portugal, gained a significant victory in 1139 at the battle of Ourique.

As time passed the silting up of the River Arade prevented ships bringing supplies and treasures to this fortress city. From 1159 the Moors' hold on the Iberian peninsula began to loosen and King Dom Sancho I of Portugal persuaded English and German Crusaders to join him in besieging Silves. Their victory in 1189 enabled the monarch to title himself King of Portugal and the Algarve, so acknowledging the province's separate identity. However his glory was short-lived, for the Moors took the city again two years later and it was several decades before the Portuguese regained control of the region. In 1249 Dom Alfonso III conquered both Silves and Faro and the Moorish resistance was finally defeated.

An age of great discovery

In 1394 King João I and his wife Philippa, daughter of the Duke of Lancaster, had their third son, Henry. He was destined to have an illustrious career. By the age of twenty-one his success fighting the Moors at Ceuta had already earned him the title Duke of Viseu. He was also to become a Grand Master of the Order of Christ and Governor of the Algarve. In fact Infante Dom Henrique (as he was known to the Portuguese) chose to retire from his father's court, taking up residence in the south-west Algarve. For a time he led a simple, monastic existence, though his active mind was soon inspired by the clear skies and open seas around Sagres. With his father's support Prince Henry gathered about him a body of cartographers, mathematicians, astronomers, navigators and adventurous sea captains. He also instructed the building of a new

Prince Henry the Navigator sits proudly on his pedestal, looking to where his brave caravels sailed out of Lagos harbour.

type of boat at the shipyards in Lagos, called a *caravel*. Its light and easily manoeuvred design was to make nautical history.

In 1420, the first period of the Great Discoveries, Prince Henry dispatched expeditions that were to benefit from the improved charts and knowledge of the sea accrued by his School of Navigation, their crews able to sail considerably further in their seaworthy caravels. His earliest success was the first landings on Porto Santo and Madeira, and later, in 1427, the discovery of the Azores. There is a nice story about his sailors' fear of the boiling seas off the African coast — their superstitions were only assuaged when one Gil Eane, born in Lagos, proved how the rough seas were actually shoals of sardines by catching them in his nets. Later he circumnavigated Cape Bojador, near the Spanish Sahara, in 1434.

Much has been written about Prince Henry the Navigator and his great contribution to Man's understanding of the planets and the quests for further knowledge of distant lands and oceans he inspired. This fine man lived to the age of sixty-five, finally being laid to rest in the Church of Santa Maria in Lagos in 1460. The great earthquake of 1755 destroyed the church, but his body was moved to the monastery of Santa Maria da Batalha, near Lisbon and also close to the graves of his royal parents.

Portuguese kings continued to support daring voyages with considerable success. In 1488 Bartolomeu Diaz rounded the Cape of Good Hope, while ten years later Vasco da Gama reached Calicut in India. In 1500 Pedro Alvares Cabral reached the coast of Brazil while Fernao de Megalhaes rounded the southern tip of South America, which he named the Magellan Straits. Despite the destruction of all but one of Magellan's five original vessels and his murder in the Phillipines, the expedition sailed on to complete the first circumnavigation of the globe in 1520. All these voyages owe their inspiration to the initiatives of Prince Henry the Navigator, as did the banks and trading posts set up according to his ideas in the new colonies.

The fate of Faro

During the sixteenth century Faro, Tavira and Lagos developed into large cities, with Faro declared as both capital and seat of bishopric. When Portugal fell under Spanish domination (1580-1640), it became drawn into the war with the English, and Faro found itself attacked by the Earl of Essex's forces. They sacked and burnt the city with such thorough destruction that only the cathedral and church of São Pedro survived. Essex plundered many works of art and religious treasures, including an important collection of archives belonging to the Bishop of Faro. This booty was given to Essex's friend Sir Thomas Bodley, who added it to his newly-founded Bodleian Library at Oxford, now one of the largest libraries in the United Kingdom.

Over the course of the next century the industrious inhabitants of Faro rebuilt their city, restoring its prestige with new churches and palaces. However their efforts were to be ruined in the eighteenth century, for three earthquakes devastated Portugal in 1719, 1722 and 1755. This last razed Lisbon itself, and Faro fared little better. The problems of these years were compounded by numerous attacks from pirates who raided up and down the Algarve coast. Nevertheless the region recovered its stature, sometimes with remarkable speed. The Algarve's most easterly town, Vila Real de Santo António, was rebuilt in only five months under the direction of the Marquis de Pombal, many of its neat houses and grids of streets still standing today.

The war against the French

During the Peninsular War Portugal was partially occupied by French forces, and the British stationed a division of Scottish Highlanders in the Algarve to prevent further invasion. Some say that certain folk dances popular in the Algarve bear an interesting similarity to the Highland Fling. In 1810 Wellington's victory at Bucaco marked the war's last major battle on Portuguese soil.

In 1807 the Portuguese Royal Family had gone into exile in Brazil, and the following year there was a revolt against the French occupation in Olhãu. Its brave citizens fought with ancient swords, sickles and stones to capture the garrison, finally flying the Portuguese flag in triumph over the local church. It is said that later two young fishermen from Olhãu sailed all the way to Brazil in a caique some 20m in length to tell the King that the French forces had been expelled. Since then Olhão has always been known as the 'Village of Independence'.

The next decades were a time of political upheaval for the Portuguese, with constant struggles between the monarchy and supporters of constitutional reform. Towards the end of the nineteenth century there was a move towards republicanism, and on 1 February 1908 an assassin murdered King Carlos and his eldest son as they rode through Lisbon. His second son, Prince Manuel, was only wounded and assumed the throne, though with little success. By 1910 rising Republican agitation and a revolt by the military culminated in his deposition. King Manuel II, the last King of Portugal, sought exile in Britain and died at Twickenham, England in 1932.

The twentieth century

Political chaos followed the monarchy's overthrow until well after the First World War, which Portugal entered on the side of the Allies. A revolution in 1926 brought power to General Antonio Oscar de Fragosa Carmona, and six years later his finance minister, Antonio de Oliveira Salazar became Prime Minister. His dictatorial regime lasted over thirty years, and was only terminated in 1968 when he suffered a stroke. His successor was Dr Marcelo Caetano, who relaxed some of the governmental controls that had constricted the nation. Six years later the armed forces seized control in the spectacular revolution of 25 April 1974. It was an important day for Portuguese politics, marking the end of dictatorship and a chance for new democratic freedoms.

The modern marina of Vilamoura provides moorings for yachts and cruisers from many foreign countries.

One of the first moves by the nation's new rulers was to grant independence to its colonies around the world. For some the transition was peaceful, but in others, notably Angola and East Timor, there was considerable bloodshed. Over a million refugees returned to Portugal with a good many settling in the Algarve, an influx that created a shortage of jobs and homes. Despite political and economic problems the new democracy has survived to create a rising standard of living for its citizens.

By the late 1970s Portugal was ready to benefit from the package holiday boom that swept through Europe, and the warm sunshine of the Algarve made it a popular destination for holidaymakers. In time some visitors chose to stay, building villas and establishing businesses. Gradually the cobble streets were paved over and new hotels started to rise alongside sandy beaches. Such developments created new employment for the many Portuguese who had previously won a meagre living from the land. The young forsook the country way of life, learning quickly how to cater for their new visitors. They soon profited, and so the people of the Algarve began to take their place in the modern world.

The Algarve today

As Portugal is now a member of the EEC the Algarve has benefited from the financial grants awarded to the country. A large proportion of these funds have been allocated to improve roads and instal mains water and drainage. As a consequence the countryside, particularly around the tourist areas and along main routes, is in turmoil. In addition to these essential improvements there are new apartments, villas and shopping precincts springing up in every town, so it's no wonder if today's visitors grow disenchanted with the region's modern face. Be patient, the chaos that now surrounds Portimão, Praia da Rocha and Albufeira will subside and with the eventual planting of trees and shrubs the whole area will take on a pleasant vista.

The discerning traveller has only to make a short journey of a few kilometres to the north of these seaside resorts to find another world. Inland lie peaceful farms where orchards of almonds, peaches, apricots, oranges and lemons cover the land. In many places the fields are still tilled with rudimentary implements and the harvest is gathered by hand. It is a fascinating sight to see an olive tree being beaten with a long cane, the olives falling onto a cloth below to be picked up by hand.

In general it is the older generations that remain in the countryside, content to live off the land of their forefathers. With improved transport and education their sons and daughters now make for the towns to work in businesses and shops, or as part of the Algarve's tourist industry. Only at weekends or for fiestas and holidays will they return to the farmlands and a family reunion.

The Algarvians are a kindly people, polite and helpful to their fellows and possessing a good sense of humour. In our opinion they are rarely intrusive, even to the extent that they often appear indifferent to passing visitors, preferring to respond only when approached.

Thankfully the true character of the Algarvian *velhote* (peasant) has remained intact, despite the annual invasion of the region by foreign holidaymakers and itinerant workers from nearby Andalusia. In this age of rush and race it's good to know that here in the southwest edge of Europe live a people whose values remain sound.

Language

In the Algarve the people speak Portuguese, which is said to be a beautiful and poetic language derived from Latin. Despite that it sounds like an Eastern European language when spoken, though it looks very similar to Spanish when written.

A general rule of spoken Portuguese is to accent the penultimate syllable, unless the accent is indicated elsewhere. The Algarvians include their own special dialect, which does not make it easier for the foreign tourist. Fortunately English is widely spoken and it can be said that few problems arise through not being able to speak Portuguese.

A Portuguese/English vocabulary of the more common words likely to be encountered is given at Appendix A.

Agriculture

The Algarve is divided into three natural regions. To the north lies the Serra region, which consists of ancient schist rocks and forms a high barren steppe of poor soil, amid mountain peaks. The middle region, called the Barrocal, benefits from the fact that water is more abundant so allowing arboriculture, with trees such as the almond, olive and carob producing useful crops which make an economical profit on a small scale.

Around the urban centre of Silves some fields of maize and rice are grown. Rock salt is mined near Loulé. An interesting fact is that sea salt is also collected in the wet lands by Castro Marim.

It is in the low fertile valleys along the flat coastal region that the main crops are grown. Attractive groves of citrus fruits spread across the land together with vineyards and horticulture. Melons, tomatoes, strawberries, vegetables, salad crops and flowers all do well, so helping the economy.

Milking cows are usually kept in barns and only bullocks are put out to pasture, owing to lack of grass. Mules and donkeys are still used in the more remote northern parts. One of the exceptions is at Vilamoura, east of the urban area, where 375 acres of prime pasture land with 600 cattle produce 5,000 litres of milk a day. Here also are 40 acres of vineyards.

Industry

Fishing

Although the tourist trade has become such an important factor in the economy of the Algarve, fishing still contributes in a large way, as it has done over the past centuries. The Algarve has always been known as Portugal's 'province of the sea', with three quarters of its boundary facing the ocean.

It is recorded that the Phoenicians were probably the first to observe the annual migration of the huge tunny (thunnus Thynnus) from the open seas of the Atlantic to the inshore waters close to the south coast of the Algarve in May and June, and their return along the same route in July and August. These clever people devised traps to ensnare the great fish and for years the same design of trap was used and called *armacoes de atum*. Much has been written about the past sea battles for these strong fish, some of which weigh over 1,000 lb (455 kilos). Brave Algarvian fishermen, having caught the tunny in their nets, then had to harpoon them and heave their great weight on to the decks, the sea running with blood. Such was the fearsome scene, 'the bullfight of the sea', that people on shore would come from afar to watch and encourage their fisher folk.

Nowadays with larger fishing boats and modern electronic equipment the tunny is caught further out at sea, with less strain on the fishermen and, one hopes, a quicker end for the mighty tunny. If you wish to see a catch being brought ashore, then make a visit to Portimão harbour.

Cod *(bacalha)* is caught in quantity and often dried and salted away for use in winter. Olhão is where you will see cod and other catches being auctioned in the huge undercover fish market.

The sardine has been the piscatorial emblem of the province of the Algarve for many years, and at most fish stalls you will see the shiny silver fishes that look so much larger before they are tinned. Quite one of the nicest meals is to have fresh sardines, rolled in salt and grilled over a charcoal fire, with crispy, fresh baked bread and a glass of *vinho*.

In the past salt pans close to the fishing ports allowed much of the fish to be preserved in salt for shipment to other countries. The first plant for pressure cooking fish and packing in tins was inaugurated in 1865 at Vila Real de Santo António. As well as tuna and sardines, anchovies *(biqueirao)* are canned and exported. The latest development in this fishing saga, is the deep freezing method, where the fish are frozen at sea; this includes shellfish, so that today's supermarkets always have a selection of frozen seafoods for all to enjoy.

Fishing trawlers alongside the quay at Vila Real de Santo António

Cork

The evergreen cork is still a source of income and it is interesting to see these large and beautiful trees being stripped. The bark is remarkably elastic, compressible and impervious to moisture. This is why ageing bottles of wine always have cork stoppers.

It takes the tree about twenty years to reach maturity. The first stripping is made at midsummer, when the trunk has shrunk from the outer bark in the dry season. Cuts are made around the trunk, then vertical cuts to penetrate the cork bark without harming the surface of the inner tree. This is a highly skilled job. The semi ridged circular portions of cork are boiled in water for eight to 10 hours to make them flexible enough to be piled flat. They are then taken to factories to be manufactured into a variety of commodities. You may be able to visit a cork factory in Silves.

Once the outer bark of the tree is removed, the exposed surface is a brilliant orange colour. It is a wonderful sight to pass a grove of cork oaks after stripping. The surface colour of the tree gradually changes from orange to brown and then greyish black as the new cork growth develops. An average tree yields about twelve strippings in its life of 70 to 150 years. The final product is charcoal and 'Spanish black', used to colour the faces of 'coal black mamas' in theatrical shows.

Basketry

The making of baskets as a cottage industry has vastly reduced in recent years. When making a purchase be sure that it is not an import from China or elsewhere. The local material used is either strips of palm *(palmita),* esparto grass *(stipa tenacissma)* or rushes *(juncus var).*

The strips of *palmita* fronds are soaked in water to soften them before being plaited and sewn together. The structure is sometimes stiffened with cane from willows *(salix fragilis)* which grow by the river banks. Monchique and Aljezur are centres for basket making.

With the coming of the tourist trade there has been an increase in the number of basketry souvenir items, such as hats, little donkeys, trays and lamp shades. These are not too heavy to transport by air.

Knitting

Once lace-making was a regular pastime for the womenfolk of the Algarve, but with the coming of tourism and modern ways the craft is rarely practised by the young and it is difficult to purchase genuine handmade lace now. However during the dark winter evenings knitting is still done and amongst the stalls at the markets you may be able to find a hand knitted heavy pullover to buy from the original knitter (look at the seams to see that it is not machine made). These garments are light, warm and usually not expensive.

Music and dancing

The Algarvíos enjoy music and dancing which are an important part of their fiestas and family gatherings. The origin of many of the songs and dances derives from several influences over past years. The influence of foreign troops — in particular the English and French — has added to the Moorish and Spanish rhythms.

The *baile mandado* is a form of dance probably of Scottish origin. In this dance the mandador guides the dancers with rhyming words and satirical comments. The *corridinho* is a dance 'of the people', similar to the polka rhythm, very fast with stamping feet and whirling skirts. Another popular dance is the *tia anica do Loulé,* a ring dance (or square dance) where couples perform a special set of energetic dance steps, with a sort of rivalry between the interchanging couples. A large number of dances have the rhythm of the mazurka. The songs are usually about popular legends, or work in the fields, and fishing. They are mostly sung in a light-hearted and airy manner.

Folklore shows are staged regularly in the big hotels and they are cheerful entertainment, with the dancers usually inviting the audience to participate. The girls wear black felt hats at a tilted angle, over a coloured headscarf, white blouses and striped skirts with white aprons, often trimmed with lace. High button shoes go over white stockings. In the swirling movement of the dances, the sight of many layers of underwear, including lacy, knee length pants, provokes much merriment. The men are soberly attired in white shirts, red kerchief, black waistcoat, black trousers with coloured cummerbund and black felt hat. The singers and dancers are accompanied by accordians and triangles.

Fado singing, the sad troubador songs of the Middle Ages, is traditional Portuguese music and not specially related to the Algarve region.

The Hotel Eva in Faro offers lively folk music of the Algarve every Thursday evening. Faro has a strong cultural importance as several music festivals of international level are held there every year. The Spring Music Week and Holy Concerts are held in the Cathedral, where the mighty pipe organ is heard. In July and August the Algarve Musical Summer Festival has a programme of music performed by orchestras, soloists, choruses and musical ensembles of high repute.

Festivals

Throughout the Algarve every town has a festival at least once a year, either of a religious or popular nature. The religious *festa* is in the form of solemn processions when images decorated with fresh flowers are paraded slowly through the streets on a wooden litter, often being taken from one religious place to another. A large number of people take part including local dignitaries and members of brotherhoods, military and police forces, seamen's organisations, fire services, boy scouts and many brass bands.

In Faro, impressive and solemn evening processions are held during Holy Week. On the second Sunday after Easter, Loulé holds the Romaria e Festa da Máe Soberana which has its origins in both pagan and Christian traditions. Fairs *(feiras),* although still typical and traditional, now incorporate modern commercial aspects and include funfairs and amusements. The city of Faro's Feira do Carmo (July) and Feira de Santa Iria (October), with Loulés famous Carnival (February) are times when the people of the Algarve put aside their cares. All the houses and streets are decorated with paper ornaments and flowers. Everyone dresses in their best clothes and there is much merriment; at night the sky is lit with fireworks. Musicians playing regional instruments roam the streets and flower battles create much excitement.

Should you happen to be in the Algarve at such times, you will be able to participate. An up-to-date list of festivities can be obtained from a Tourist Information Office (see page 62.)

Flora

The beautiful countryside of the Algarve, with its mild climate of hot summers and wet winters, can be a botanist's paradise. It is a riot of colour from January until the heat of summer dries the land.

It is true to say that here spring comes in January, when the almond trees blossom, whole orchards of pink and white buds make the air fragrant and the countryside a wonderful sight. Mimosa, too, flowers early in the year as does the invasive yellow oxalis seen along the hedgerows and edges of fields. From February onwards the little yellow celandine blooms in sandy places and the crocus-like *romulea bulbocdium* can be found. By March many wild flowers greet the eye. The grape hyacinth *(muscari alanticum),* with its dark flowers, is seen on hills and fields. Along the cliffs and sandy places the sea pink *(armeria pungens)* spreads its pink flowering cover. The wellknown asphodelus stands tall and elegant on banks and verges. Out in the far western countryside around Sagres, on windswept land, the sturdy French lavender *(lavendula stoechas)* grows in large patches of purple bracts, its fragrance pervading the air. Along the western region, too, whole areas of uncultivated countryside are covered by the sticky bushes of the cistus family, another aromatic plant.

Early February is the time when the almond blossom heralds the coming of spring.

By April most of the wild flowers are in bloom and it is a pleasant surprise to see the blue Love-in-the-Mist *(nigella arvensis)* and the field gladioli *(gladiolus segetum)* with the pretty little iris *(iris sisyrinchium)* growing amongst the long grasses. Orchids, too, can be spotted: the Bumble Bee orchid *(ophrys bombliflora)* and the Minor Orchid *(ophrys speculum)*, a wonderful sight with its vivid blue centre lip. More easily found is the well-known borage *(borago officinalis)*. These are only some of the many varieties found here. Charles Wuepel in his book *The Algarve* (see Bibliography) states that he had identified 1,200 species and goes into detail of the flora to be found in very distinctive zones.

Mention must be made of the interesting evergreen arbutus, or strawberry tree *(arbutus unedo)*, called *medronhiera* in Portuguese. The berries ripen in autumn and look very similar to strawberries. Gathered, they are used to make a very strong liqueur, Medronho. It is also possible to put them in a fruit pie. As one drives on the EN120 from Lagos to Barranco de Vaca, you see plenty of these trees growing on the roadside.

Travelling from the coast up to the Monchique mountains, trees dominate the scenery — great cork oaks, eucalyptus, olive, sweet chestnuts and plane trees. On the route to Fóia the *camella japonica* trees bloom in April and May. The list goes on with the holly oak *(quercus coccifer)* and the attractive European palm *(chamaerops humilis)*.

In the wetter places ferns, mosses and lichen cling to the banks of the streams. In gardens and orchards the orange, lemon, peach, apple, pear and fig trees are abundant. Where water is readily available cottages and villas are a lovely riot of colour from the brilliant blooms. The hibiscus, arum lilies, creeping geraniums, bougainvillaea and bignonia climb the terraces. By the coast, hotels and apartment blocks soften the modern architecture with great displays of tropical plants, rock gardens, cactus and prickly pear. Finally there are the wild herbs like sage, thyme and rosemary, which perfume the air.

Do spare time to explore and enjoy the immense variety of flora found in the Algarve.

Wildlife

Today there are few fierce wild animals in the Algarve, where once the wolf *(lobo)* roamed the mountains. Both badger and fox are rare but sometimes a ring-tailed civet cat *(gato de algália)* can cause havoc in a poultry farm. Both hare *(lebre)* and rabbit *(coelho)* are hunted with a gun or ferret *(ferao)* and the meat is eaten.

The only venomous snake of the Algarve is the snub nosed viper *(vipera latastei boscá)* or *vibra*. This can be found in the rocky dry mountainous areas. Several non-poisonous snakes appear in the hot summer, the most common being the horseshoe snake *(coluber hippocrepis),* so called because of the dark band across the base of its head which curves down the neck; it also has yellow spots and a belly marked red, orange and yellow. You are likely in midsummer to see lizards: the green one *(lagarto verde)* and the eyed lizard *(lacerta lepida),* which can be 45cm long. There are plenty of chameleons, salamanders and the shy geckos, who like to sun themselves on warm rocks, only to dart away at the slightest movement.

Butterflies, dragonflies, moths and many other winged creatures, enjoy the warm climate and green countryside of the Algarve.

Birds

Because of the varied landscape and vegetation there is plenty to interest the birdwatcher in the Algarve. Sparrows, swallows, martins and robins are a familiar sight to British eyes. Corn buntings, linnets, swifts, warblers, chiff chaffs, blackcaps, mistle thrush, blackbirds and nightingales are to be heard and often seen. The list is long but you are likely to observe kestrels, larks and, in the oak forests, the brilliant hoopoe, golden oriole, green woodpecker and many other birds. Birds of prey include eagles, black vultures and buzzards. The quail and red-legged partridge are the game birds.

In the Sotavento salt marshes and mudflats, flocks of black headed gulls, avocets and godwits are seen together with sanderlings, dunlins and plovers. The delightful little white egrets and grey herons often feed along the water beds of the causeway to Faro beach.

As well as the famous ravens near Cabo São Vicente lighthouse, along the Barlavento coast, you are likely to notice herring gulls and black-backed gulls, gannets, Cory's shearwaters, guillemots, razorbills and jackdaws. If you are fortunate you will also see the great white storks *(cegonha)* nesting, usually on church towers. Look for the nest above the old city gate in Faro.

Nature reserves

Castro Marim Nature Reserve

This is a vast region between the village of Castro Marim and the Rio Guadiana, a natural habitat of birds, fish and rare wild plants. It is swampy marshland of much ecological interest, particularly as such areas are disappearing. Because there is no pollution, this place is a natural breeding ground for numerous crabs and oysters.

Parque National da Ria Formosa

South of Faro and Olhão and offshore is an area of immense ecological importance, created by the silting of the coastline; various lagoons and small islands have been formed. Because most of this area is unfit for habitation it has been declared a wild life sanctuary and much is being done to preserve the rare specimens of plants, birds and seashore creatures. The area extends from Ançao to Cacela Velha, a distance of about 55km facing the sea, and a total area of 17,000 hectares, containing dunes, inlets and islands. It is a place rich in shell fish and where many fish species lay their eggs. Migratory birds stop over, which is of interest to ornithologists.

Portuguese water dog

The Portuguese water dog is a recognised breed, whose origins go back into history. Originally its main use was to herd sheep, but with the increase of the Portuguese fishing fleets, especially in the Algarve, new uses were found for this hard-working dog. In appearance it is mainly black, with short curly coat, and in size it resembles a Newfoundland. Some have white feet and a long tail tuft of white.

As a fisherman's dog it went to sea. It is a strong swimmer and often it was used to retrieve tackle and chase the fish into the nets. In fog the fishermen used to make the dogs bark so that they could keep in touch with the rest of the fleet; also the dogs could swim from boat to boat with messages. If sharks were about the dogs seemed to know and gave warning. On the quay they were ferocious guard dogs and no one could get past them on to the boats.

This courageous and handsome dog is also a good family dog, being devoted to its master. Nowadays, their brave service is no longer required with modern fishing trawlers and they have become popular as pets. In America there is a thriving Portuguese Water Dog Club. An interesting book about dogs, written by Kathryn Braund and Deyanne Farrell Millar (see bibliography) was published in 1986. It contains many photographs showing the dogs at work.

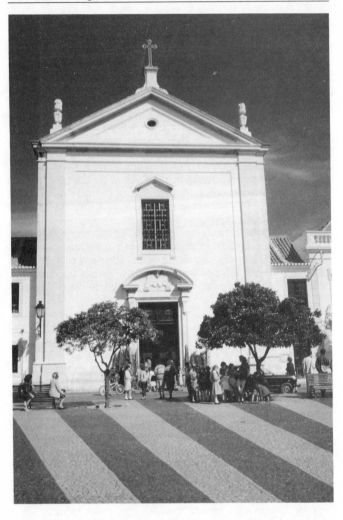

The simple lines of the parish church in Vila Real de Santa António show up clearly, against the blue sky and black and white striped square, where the orange trees provide some shade.

TEN

Eastern Algarve: Vila Real to Olhao

For the purpose of easy reading the following road tours are described in an east to west direction, with some short excursions off the main highway. Inland routes are detailed in a separate chapter. The distance between Vila Real de Santo António and Cape St Vincent in the west is relatively short (108 miles/173 kms), and wherever you are staying visits to places of interest can be made in either direction. The chapters which follow aim to give visitors some knowledge of what to expect when touring Portugal's province of the Algarve.

From Vila Real to the Alentejo border

Throughout the year many visitors enter the Algarve by taking the car ferry from Ayamonte in the south east of Spain (Seville 100 miles/160 kms), crossing the Rio Guadiana to Vila Real de Santo António. During the day these open deck ferries go to and fro in a steady stream carrying vehicles and foot passengers. A large proportion of travellers are day trippers wishing to make shopping expeditions. It is well to remember that these ferries can become extremely busy, particularly on public holidays, especially with Portuguese families travelling over to Ayamonte in search of cheaper household goods. Unfortunately, it is not possible to make an advance booking. However, on both sides of the river the queue is orderly and you must hope that you do not cross at the same time as the busy tourist coaches. By the Vila Real port office and customs there is a useful Tourist Information Office where you can change money and collect details about the local area. It is open on Sunday.

Vila Real de Santo António
This town is a very pleasant place to visit, it has a quiet and gracious atmosphere, with the advantage of plenty of car parking space along

the river esplanade, which is close to the centre of the town. Horse-drawn carriages parked along the front are for hire and this is a leisurely way to explore.

The eighteenth-century town that you see today was constructed by the order of the Marquis de Pombal in 1774. It was built on the site of the former Santo António de Arenilha which was washed away by the sea in the sixteenth century. Because the land was flat and arid the new town was completed in just five months, which must have been a considerable feat for those days. It is said that some of the stonework was brought from Lisbon. Vila Real (Royal Town) is built in parallel lines around a central square, which is surrounded on four sides by classical style two and three storey buildings, similar to those of the Baixa in Lisbon. In the main square, black and white mosaic tiles radiate in wedges outwards from a central obelisk while tall graceful black wrought-iron street lamps add to the charm of this spacious square, which is called **Praça do Marques do Pombal.**

During the winter and early spring the scent of the orange blossom and the bright fruit on the trees that line each side of the square give it a rural atmosphere. Old folk dressed in black sit on the benches watching their grandchildren at play. While the fishermen are away at sea, their wives are probably at work in the nearby hotels and shops. On one side of the square the two hundred and ten year old white **church** is slightly taller than other buildings. The interior is cool with four beautiful stained glass windows and a serene Madonna with white hand-made lace handkerchief.

It is an interesting fact that in the Algarve the clergy have to work for a living, not being supported by the Church.

If you are in the square between 1700 and 1900 hrs it is well worth visiting the **Museu Manuel Cabanas,** entrance is free. This is a unique little museum, because it features the life work of one man, Manuel Cabanas, a printer and engraver of high repute, who was born in Vila Real. It is a small treasure house of rare editions and engravings with the metal cuts, woodcarvings and tools necessary for the intricate work. Of unusual interest are the large marble printing stamps, used in the past to make the designs for the top of many different tuna and sardine tins. The art work is amazingly intricate. Some modern paintings have added to this historical collection and they are inclined to jar the senses if you felt transported to a different era by the painstaking work of Manuel Cabanas.

If you look at the road map of Vila Real you will notice that, even today the streets are amazingly symmetrical, which makes it easy to find your way around. Most of the shops lie along the river front, **Avenida da Republica,** and close to the central square. A number of the small shops are full of bric-a-brac and fancy goods for tourists to buy. However, on the outskirts of Vila Real, on Rua 25th Abril (the road leading to Monte Gordo) there is a large emporium called **Paga Pouco.** Here prices are reasonable with best buys being the Portuguese products like tablecloths, bedspreads, knitwear and colourful Portuguese pottery. Some of the clothes and footwear can be a bargain.

Across the road, almost opposite, is a marble factory and if you are not too intrusive, the workers may allow you to look around this dusty and noisy place, but you will have to return to Paga Pouco to purchase your marble souvenir.

Along Avenida da Republica, the long river front, you will notice at each end two old **turrets,** a reminder of the pirate era of the past. A few fishing boats still use the docks, mainly unloading sardines for the canning factories. Here too excursion boats depart with holidaymakers for a trip up and down the broad **Rio Guadiana.** The banks of the river have been declared a nature park. Ornithologists

A fine example of the gracious houses built by order of the Marquis de Pombal at Vila Real.

will delight in the amount of water fowl and birds to be seen in the shallow sandy reeds, which are also the habitat of many shellfish and crustaceans — oysters, shrimps, crabs, whelks and lobster. Fishing, too, is popular and you are likely to catch grey mullet and barbel, along the sandy bottomed river line of this estuary. It is also a favourable place to find bass, sole and plaice. At the northen end of the waterfront is Vila Real's railway station, and inland from there on the Rua de Angola, is the Bullring.

Castro Marim, an ancient settlement

Although Vila Real de Santo António is now the most south-eastern frontier town with Spain, in the past primitive man inhabited the high land some four kilometres to the north at **Castro Marim.** This has been proven by finds from the Neolithic period and metals from a pre-historic fortified area. The Phoenicians probably founded the present settlement and had a port there, too. During the Arab domination it was an important trading base and a large part of the old Muslim castle still remains. After the Christian conquest it became part of the so called Kingdom of the Algarve, receiving its municipal charter in the year 1277. The circular walls of the Christian castle became, in 1319, the home of the Military Order of Christ (which succeeded the disbanded Knights Templar).

The order was transferred to Tomar, north of Lisbon, in 1335. The fortifications of the castle were constantly strengthened and in the seventeenth century a second fort was built. Much of this castle still remains, although it was partially damaged in the earthquake of 1755. With the building of Vila Real, Castro Marim's importance declined as the people moved into the fine new town nearby.

Today, Castro Marim is beginning to be discovered and developed into a tourist attraction. A particularly pleasant way to explore this little backwater town is to take a buggy ride from Vila Real. These horse drawn carriages with their elderly Algarvío drivers, take four passengers, unless you are young enough to sit up front and help with the reins. As you clip clop along at a smart pace, you have time to take in the gentle countryside that lies between Vila Real and Castro Marim. Much of this area is marshy and rich in flora and fauna, it being part of the Castro Marim Nature Reserve. Here you may see little egrets, storks, oyster catchers, golden plovers, snipe, kingfishers, divers, herons and marsh eagles. Many migratory birds nest here, too. You will have a chance to photograph the saltpans in various stages of salt production, from the dry salt beds to the huge pyramids of salt waiting to be collected for refining and exporting. In the spring time many wild flowers grow along the verges of the country road called Rua Combatentes da Grande Guerra. Incidentally, when the buggy reaches a hill the male tourists may be required to get out and walk!

Arriving at Castro Marim you are sure to be impressed with the sight of the two large castles each set on hills either side of the tiny town that nestles safely between these ancient fortresses. The oldest castle, **Fort Sáo Sebastiano** Tiao, has a striking outline because of its high entrance. Apparently, it was a place of execution, and it certainly looks as if it was made high enough for a gibbet or guillotine.

Narrow, cobbled and winding streets have small and picturesque houses in the older part of town. See how tiny are some of the doorways, and note the attractive and colourful patterned glazed tiles that cover many of the front walls. Look, too, at the round key point on the outside wall of each house. These were to enable the landlord to turn off the water supply if the bill was not paid!

To reach the ancient castle, which now belongs to the National Trust, you will need to park your car (if that is how you travelled) in the public carpark and walk up a fairly steep, cobbled incline. Disabled visitors taking it slowly will find the effort rewarding as they look down onto the red roofs of the village below. With a bit of searching you may discern where an artistic villager has painted on a wall a large map of the whole of the Algarve.

Once inside the castle walls you will want to visit the Tourist Information Office and investigate some of the excavations, then explore a second castle, **Castelo Velho.** This is built on a square plan with four towers and two doors, and much of it has been restored. Inside this second castle is part of a ruined church, with a carved wooden altar which dates from the sixteenth century. Still inside you enter the **Archaeological Museum,** spaciously laid out with interesting items, like old tools and muskets relating to the history of Castro Marim.

Outside again the energetic will want to climb the rough stone steps leading to the circular ramparts, from where you can admire the extensive views over the flat countryside below and see the distant lighthouse on the coast. Binoculars will help you see the Spanish frontier town of Ayamonte lying across the Rio Guadiana. Its white buildings stand out brightly against the blue sky and you may even be able to discern the storks' nests on the huge church tower.

Returning to the streets below the castle you may be fortunate and find the doors of the white **Church of Nossa Senhora dos Martires** open. Of eighteenth-century origin it has an interesting dome with a Moorish look. An annual pilgrimage takes place here on 15 August, when the Holy Image is taken in procession to a nearby hermitage. There are only a few shops in Castro Marim and even fewer eating places, but Vila Real is but a short drive away from where you can enjoy tasty seafood dishes of shrimps, crab, cockles, oysters, lamprey, grilled sardines, golden bream and grey mullet.

Alcoutim and beyond

Continuing further north, the N122 is a fairly good road that winds gently amongst sweet perfumed pine trees and open farmland, making a pleasant drive. In places the ground is a mass of wild shrubs so colourful in spring; the gum cistus, with their huge fluttering white flowers, the blue and white iris, the tall pink and white asphodelus and the delicate and fragrant French lavendar. When you fancy a quiet country drive, this is where you should head for and maybe stop on the roadside for a picnic. You will pass by or through the small villages of **Monte Francisco, Junqueira** and **Azinhal.** If you are there on market day you will find only a few simple wares for sale, like shoes, jumpers, metal jugs, buckets and country tools, laid out on odd bits of cloth. The twentieth century has hardly reached these less populated inland villages. You will see the hard working Algarve peasants still toiling with their hands, removing piles of stones from the dry soil of their farmland.

The road continues to **Odelite,** where perhaps you will see a local basket-maker sitting by the roadside weaving his wares. If you stop to get out your video camera, chances are that he will continue his work without so much as a glance at you. The Portuguese are, generally speaking, a shy people who do not make overtures to tourists, but they will acknowledge your wave. The drive now takes you towards the mountains and larger vistas come into view. At Corte de Seda a turning east on the N122 -1 road takes you a further six kilometres to **Alcoutim** which is 40km (25 miles) from Castro Marim. Park in the tiny village square, by the village stores. A small restaurant can provide you with a meal. It is pleasant to walk down to the river, and across the water you will clearly see the white washed buildings and church of the Spanish town of Sanlucar de Guadiana. This Portuguese frontier crossing is for foot passengers only, as the small ferry boat does not take vehicles.

Alcoutim's history goes back a long way, it had a Roman presence here. Conquered by Dom Sancho II in 1240, the castle was rebuilt and strengthened against a possible Spanish invasion from across the river. Over the years this fortification has fallen into disuse, as its requirement lessened, but its sturdy battlements are a reminder of Portugal's turbulent history. Rarely visited by tourists is the **Igreja de Nossa Senhora da Conceiçao,** the matriarcial church. In 1876 this sturdy church, built on a hill, was the refuge for the homeless people of the village when the Rio Guadiana flooded its banks. Now you are likely to see a stork nesting on the bell tower.

If you wish to extend your drive, you can return from Alcoutim by the same route to the main N122 road and then continue 10kms (6 miles) north, until you reach the north/eastern border of the Algarve province with the Alentejo.

You should allow one and a half hours for your return journey to Vila Real. Going downhill towards the sea seems to be quicker than when you were going north and stopping on the way for sightseeing.

Monte Gordo and the beaches

Vila Real de Santo António to Monte Gordo is a distance of five kilometres. There are two routes you can take. The main EN125 to Faro goes past the fire station in Vila Real then branches off to the south and leads into the back of Monte Gordo. This is the route the bus takes. A more attractive drive is to leave Vila Real via the Rua 25 de Abril, past the Paga Pouca shop and drive slowly along the coastal road going through thick pinewoods. Seawards is the beginning of the vast sandy beach that is the reason for Monte Gordo becoming such a popular holiday venue. At the beginning of the **Monte Gordo** development an extensive area in the pinewoods on the land side of the road is taken up by a large camping ground, **Parque Municipal de Campismo Monte Gordo.** (see Chapter 4, Camping). This is a destination for many British and international campers, and it is especially busy during the winter months with long stay caravanners. In the summer campers from Spain arrive. Practically opposite to the camp entrance are large carparks.

The **Casino Monte Gordo,** which is open from 1700 to 0300 hrs every day, is an added attraction to this restful seaside town. Seven hotels, three pensions and two apartment blocks are modern high rise buildings and used by several British package tour operators.

The town has a good choice of bars, cafés and restaurants that range from the simple snack bar to more elegant establishments. Apart from the hotels, eating places and a small selection of souvenir and everyday shops, a post office and a bank, there is little of interest in Monte Gordo. The original village, which lies at the back of the modern development, until recently housed a poor Portuguese community. It is only with the expansion of tourism that housing conditions have improved for the local inhabitants. Buses, taxis and horsedrawn carriages are to be found along the seafront as well as the Tourist Information Office. Excursions can be made from Monte Gordo, by coach, to Faro, Lisbon and Seville.

Sunseeking holidaymakers go to Monte Gordo because it has an enormous, flat beach of wide, golden sand, with clear seas for swimming, sailing and surfing. There are sun umbrellas, *pedalos* and beach bars and a number of gaily painted, small fishing boats add to the idyllic scene. This eastern end of the Algarve provides a quieter holiday venue than the busier resorts of Albufeira, Praia da Rocha and further west.

This bird's eye view of the wonderful, wide beach at Monte Gordo also shows the Casino on the left and several beach bars.

Driving westwards out of Monte Gordo on the EN125 you soon reach a road sign directing you south to **Praia do Alemao,** which is a continuation of the Monte Gordo beach. At **Praia Verde,** another beach entrance has low umbrella pinetrees which reach right to the edge of the sand dunes, offering some shade from the midday sun. Here, too, is another large camping park called Campismo Torralta (see Chapter 4, Camping). This part of the beach is favoured by windsurfers.

The next beach resort is at **Praia Manta Rota** 12km (7.5 miles) from Monte Gordo, and it is still the same golden beach that beckons. This one is popular with Algarvian families who like to use the restaurant and snack bar, O Estabulo, which has a playground on the beach.

Continuing on, at 16kms (10 miles) from Monte Gordo we reach **Vila Nova de Cacela,** situated either side of the EN125. It is said to have been a Phoenician settlement, later occupied by the Romans and conquered from the Moors in 1240. Today its inhabitants take little notice of passing tourists and go about their daily work in a sober manner. The red soil of the countryside around here is attractively covered with apple, orange and olive groves. Low built houses have climbing plants and trellises covered with the bright hues of bougainvillea and orange fire bignonia. Inland, across the railway line at Calico is a rural campsite.

Again, just off the main EN125, south at Cacela, are more sand dunes and a lagoon. **Cabanas** is a new development with modern apartment blocks and pensions. There are sports facilities, bars and restaurants. Boat trips can be made across the lagoon to the isolated barrier beaches where sea birds, storks and white egrets can be seen.

Tavira, city of churches

You are now approaching Tavira, surrounded by well tended agricultural land, where some vineyards and citrus fruit orchards flourish. In spring time the almond blossom creates a pink and white haze across the fields. The pink flowers are the bitter almonds, the white the sweet almonds. The carob tree is another that is planted along most of the southern part of the Algarve. The long, large beans are used for chocolate flavouring and the husks make animal fodder. **Tavira** is an important city that lies close to the EN125 main road 30kms (19 miles) east of Faro. Its many churches, spires and domes make a notable landmark against the blue sky. Historically, Tavira was at one time the biggest city of the Algarve. You can still see today the old Roman stone bridge, with its seven arches, spanning the Rio Gilao.

In 1242 Dom Paio Peres Correia and his men finally brought the town under Christian rule, their attack came as a revenge for the murder, by the Moors, of seven Christian knights. In 1266 the town received its charter and in 1520 was raised to the status of City. At that time it was much sought after for its port, by large ships to and from the Mediterranean. For a while it thrived, but in 1645 a plague wiped out many of its population and then in 1755, more disaster, when much of the city was destroyed in a terrible earthquake. Because of the gradual silting up of the harbour its importance as a port has declined and today only a few vessels use its facilities. Known as the Venice of the Algarve, the present city is divided by the **Rio Gilao,** with some fine nineteenth century houses lining the eastern bank. On the western bank of the river, a rather splendid esplanade has nicely laid out public gardens with neat box hedges. The stall **market** and **amusement park** are close by. Down by the mouth of the river are some salt pans.

Tavira has many crafts-people who produce souvenirs made of cork, decorative objects from shells, regional style blouses and lace articles. A pretty product are the colourful flowers made from paper, but they need to be boxed to get them safely home. Further handicrafts are rope mats, reed baskets and wooden chairs: these are exported. A visit to Tavira makes a pleasant contrast to the lazy days spent on the beach.

Tavira is also called the City of Churches. There are thirty seven here, with the **Santa Maria do Castelo Church** containing the tomb of Paio Peres Correia and the seven Christian knights killed by the Arabs. The **Misercórdia Church** was built in 1541; it has a stone carved Renaissance portal, flanked by two pillasters above which are the figures of St Peter and St Paul and in the middle, a little higher, is the Image of Nossa Senhora da Misercórdia. It is a very beautiful facade.

Be sure to walk up some steep steps behind the Misercórdia church and past the **Palacio de Justica** to see the pretty gardens and castle walls, then on further to the **Mirador** which overlooks the older part of the city. Here you will be able to admire the high church towers amongst the many red roofed buildings that cluster together. Along the narrow streets white washed houses have Gothic windows and doorways, some topped with coats of arms, while the round dome of a chapel is reminiscent of a Moorish mosque. In the main square **Praca da Républica** is a bus stop and taxis and in the **Rua da Galeria,** under some arches, you will see the Tourist Information Office and some art galleries. Cafés, bars and restaurants are not difficult to find. For quick service and inexpensive local cooking, try the Café Restaurant America in Rua Jose Pires Padinha 2. It is by the gardens and there is car parking.

The Thanksgiving

On the coast between Tavira and Olháo lies the fishing village of Fuseta. Their patron saint is Our Lady of Carmel, Nossa Senhora do Carmo. The dedication of the village to their patron began at least two hundred years ago.

It happened when a terrible storm blew up. In such a storm, fishermen with sailing boats are helpless unless they can find shallow water to bring the boats ashore. The fishermen's wives brought wood to make a great fire to guide their men to the safe part of the shore. Then they all knelt down in prayer and promised Our Lady of Carmel, whose feast day it was, that they would dedicate their church and village to her if the men were saved. The fishermen were able to get ashore safely and, to this day, 16 July has been a special one for the village of Fuseta.

Today, Nossa Senhora de Carmo is also paraded in August, when she is taken from the church and brought to the quayside, to await the arrival by boat from the next village of their statue, Nossa Senhora do Livramento. The two statues greet one another amidst great applause from the villagers. Then they are carried on platforms to the parish church where there is a service and High Mass, followed by another procession through the streets. This thanksgiving celebration for the safe return of their villagers is not only for fishermen who go to sea, but also for emigrants, who return from France, Germany, the Channel Islands and even America to take part in the ceremony.

On the last evening when the statue of Our Lady of Livramento is returned, by land this time, the solemn atmosphere is replaced with merry tunes and lively jigs, and a good time is had by all.

Through the Barrocal to Olhão

Two kilometres south of Tavira is **Santa Luzia,** a typical fishermen's village, with a sandy beach, where you may see octopus *(polvo)* being sold. You get a view over the lagoon, inlet and the offshore Barril and Tavira islands. In good weather these are reached by ferry boat. They are good places for a quiet picnic and a swim in warm waters. On the sea side of Tavira Island (Ilha de Tavira) there is an unofficial quiet nudist beach.

Returning to the main highway, five kilometres west of Tavira you pass through the small village of **Luz,** noted for its very curious pointed chimneys and another large sixteenth-century parish church, **Nossa Senhora da Luz.** As well as the Renaissance entrance inside the main chapel there are some very fine paintings in the vaults, while on the floor are hispano-arab glazed tiles from Seville.

The countryside around here is called the Barrocal, and since the earliest times the heavy clay soil has been used to make many types of earthenware pottery. The largest jars in the familiar 'Ali Baba' shape were made for the storage of wine and olive oil. Smaller ones have been used by the Algarvian women to carry water from the well, carefully balanced on their heads. Nowadays this clay, called **terra rosa,** is used to make the red interlocking tiles seen on so many Algarve roofs. An unusual vessel made from this clay is the *alcatruz,* an oval pot with a narrow neck, which is used to ensnare octopus. At night, these pots are connected by nylon lines to the ocean bed, where the unwary, eight tentacled octopus makes its way into this sheltered home. In the morning the pots are raised. Need I say more? For a more pleasant use there are various shapes and sizes of ornamental, red clay flower pots, but these would make rather a fragile and heavy souvenir.

Still travelling west on the EN 125, we pass by the small Sotavento fishing village of **Fuseta,** where a large percentage of the men join the cod fishing fleet at Lisbon, in April, for six months' fishing. They are amongst the best paid fishermen of the province. Down by the shores, the flat land is used as salt pans. In the summer, when the saline water has evaporated the salt crystals are gathered. Much is used locally in the fish packing stations. Here seaweed is also harvested for chemicals and as a fertiliser.

Olhão: town with a special charm

Our next place to visit is the important town of Olhão, 10kms (6 miles) east of Faro. On the eastern outskirts a sign leading towards the beach takes you to Parque dos Bancarios, a three-star campsite, by **Pinheiros de Marim** (see Chapter 4, Camping). This newly built park has up-to-date facilities and a good shop. It is used by discerning British campers as well as other nationalities. Here pinewoods lead to a sandy shore.

Olhão is a town of distinction because it has retained the look of an Arabic city. Once it was only a small fishing village, but in the late eighteenth century the development of the fishing industry, and later still the sardine and canning factories (the first one being opened here in 1882) caused the fishermen to construct houses by the port. Their connections with North Africa and the trading links with that country influenced a kasbah-style of building. Small cube-shaped, two and three storey houses were built in narrow streets. They have flat topped roofs surmounted by terraces and most of them have outside stairs leading to look-out towers *(acoteias)* that were used by the fishermen's wives on the lookout for the return of the fishing fleet — or raiding pirates.

Olhão has retained its importance as a fishing harbour, being the second largest port (after Portimão) in the Algarve. The long seafront, Avenida 5 de Outubro, is lined with sheds for selling fish and it is an interesting spectacle to watch a *lota,* the noisy fish auction. A law in the Algarve, not particularly liked by fishermen, says that all fish caught must be sold by public auction. In the same area, in a covered hall, are food and vegetable **markets.** Not all the stallholders speak English, nor do many tourists feel inclined to enter the busy scene. However, with a little commonsense and sign language, here you can shop economically and obtain really fresh fish, meat and vegetables. At the same time you can mix with the Algarvíos at work.

For children there are swings and a recreational park, **Jardim Patrao Joaquim Lopes** and, at the western end of town, a not particularly attractive beach. The bus and railway station are near the centre of Olhão, off **Avenida da Republica,** where there is a pedestrian shopping centre and Tourist Information Office. Here there are plenty of ordinary bars, cafés and a few restaurants. Nearby on the EN125 is Discoteca Joy.

Down by the **port** is the departure point for ferry boats to the islands of Armona, Culatra and Faro. Culatra is noted for its beautiful shells and is a good place for walking along the seashore.

As well as some rather ugly canning factories the town has tall apartment blocks, which tend to overshadow the older, more attractive style buildings. In the centre of town is the parish church, **Igreja Matriz.** Building began in 1698. Inside it has a Baroque style font and the fresco paintings on the ceiling are worth seeing. The Capela dos Aflitos (Chapel of Suffering) is where the fishermen's wives go to pray when there are storms at sea. It is open day and night. The nearby church, **Capela Nossa Senhora da Soledade,** has a cupola like a mosque and was built by the fishermen. One other fact about Olhão is that, as well as fish canning the production of holiday home type cane furniture has proved a lucrative industry in more recent years.

Before leaving Olhão you may care to recall the story of the small boat, Bom Sucesso, which was rowed all the way across the Atlantic Ocean to Rio de Janeiro (see Chapter 9, History) to tell the exiled King João VI that the armies of Napoleon had been driven from Portugal. Afterwards the title of Village of Independence was given to the brave people of Olhão.

It is now just 10kms (6 miles) westwards along the fast EN125 to the capital city of the Algarve, Faro.

A Tale of the Almond Blossom

Each February in the Algarve, spring comes with a haze of fragrant white almond blossom, which spreads across the countryside and reminds everyone of a certain legend.

The story goes that an Arab King, during the time the Moors ruled the Algarve, fell in love with a beautiful princess from a far off northern land. They were, for a time, happily married, but gradually the princess fell into a decline, as her nostalgia for the snows of her homeland caused her much grief. When the king heard of the reason for her great sadness he ordered a huge forest of almond trees to be planted all over the country and around the castle. The next February the sick princess was taken outside to look at the white vista below, and for the first time she smiled at her loving husband and was cured.

ELEVEN

Faro, capital of the Algarve

Situated along the Atlantic coast in an almost central position between Vila Real de Santo António in the east and Sagres to the west, the capital city of Faro is built on a lagoon which, today, is declared a Nature Reserve. Faro's modern airport is just seven kilometres to the south west. The Romans made Faro an important administrative centre: when the Christians took Faro from the Moors it became the seat of a Bishopric in the sixteenth century. The terrible earthquake of 1755 all but destroyed the walled city. It was later rebuilt and some of the old monuments restored.

Today Faro is mainly a modern city and, although at first glance it may appear somewhat faded and lacking in neatness, yet a medieval atmosphere still clings and there is much to interest visitors. Close to the lagoon a pleasant park and gardens, called **Jardim de Manuel Bivar,** allow you to sit and view the various types of architecture that line the tiny harbour. There is a useful restaurant and a kiosk here. Leading from this park you have the choice of walking to the main shopping area, much of which is restricted to pedestrians and consists of cobbled streets and narrow alleyways. Or if your interest lies in historical buildings, museums and churches, then you will head for the Old City which is situated on a hill south of the Jardim de Manuel Bivar.

The Old City

(Tour One: 2 hours) The main entrance to Faro's ancient town is south of the gardens and through the **Arco da Vila** (town arch). This imposing stone entrance was once the door to the old castle. But before exploring the Old City it is suggested that you visit the **Tourist Information Office,** which is to be found on the city side of the huge Arco da Vila. It is open Monday to Friday from 0900 to 1900 hrs and on Saturday from 0900 to 1200 hrs.

A   Railway Station
B   Harbour Master
C   Bus terminal
D   Customs
E   Fire Brigade
F   Town Hall
G   Post Office
H   Market
I   Police
J   Post Office
K   Tourist Office
L   Cathedral
M   Bishop's Palace
N   Walls of Faro

O   Arco da Vila
P   Misericórdia
Q   São Pedro Church
R   Carmo Church
S   Prince Henry R & L
          Museum
T   Maritime Museum
U   Lethes Theatre
V   Jardim de Manuel
          Bivar

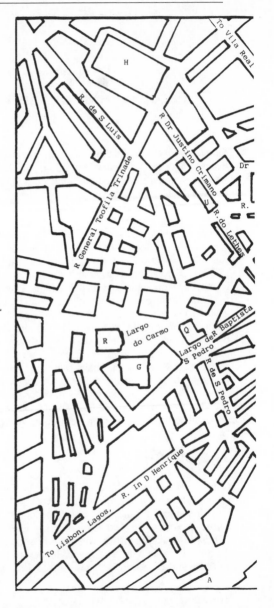

The **Arco da Vila** is an impressive white archway, built of very thick masonry and flanked by two Ionic columns, above which in a niche is a statue of St Thomas Aquinas carved in white Italian marble. It is said that St Thomas Aquinas saved the city from the plague. Yet higher you see a clock face that accurately gives the time. On the top of all this is a graceful, single bell tower capped by a weather vane. A notable feature of this tower is the nesting place of a family of storks, who return here year after year. Inside the deep Arco da Vila one can admire a beautiful Arab portico which bears witness to the fact that the city already had sturdy walls in the period of Muslim rule. The ancient brick work is a vivid link with its past history.

Once through the gateway a narrow cobbled road winds steeply uphill past ancient houses that have delicate wrought-iron balconies. At the top of the **Rua do Muncipo** you are immediately in the wide square called the **Largo da Sé**, the Cathedral Square.

The most important building in Faro both historically and architectual point of view is the great **Cathedral (Sé),** which is open to the public from Monday to Friday 0800 to 1200 hrs. Its present shape is the result of much reconstruction and restoration work. Originally thought to have been a Moorish Mosque the cathedral was built in 1251 in Romanesque Gothic style. Badly damaged by various earthquakes and by pirates, the church underwent successive changes of structure. Today its outward appearance is mighty as it stands in the peace and quiet of this lovely square above the busy city, the surrounding orange trees and old cobble stones creating a sense of tranquillity. Try and visit here early in the morning ahead of the coach parties.

Inside Faro's cathedral three naves have fine trusses, divided by six great Doric columns. Around the body of the church are beautiful polychrome glazed tiles from the eighteenth century. The tall interior has small windows and many compact side chapels, one of which is called the Chapel of Relics. It is wholly covered with intricate gilded wood carvings and amongst its treasure is a precious relic of an eighteenth-century incense boat in mother-of-pearl and silver, which belonged to Dom Joa Coutinho. The Rosary chapel is beautifully adorned with blue and white seventeenth century *azuelos* (tiles).

The richly ornate organ loft is decorated in red and gold. It was repaired a few years ago in Holland at the expense of the Calouste Gulbenkian Foundation. Well-known Portuguese and foreign organists have given concerts in the cathedral and praise the quality of the organ's tone.

This solid bronze statue of King Afonso III stands close to the Cathedral in Largo da Sé.

Behind the Cathedral at **Praça D. Afonso III,** is the former convent of **Nossa Senhora de Assuncão,** also known as the Nun's Convent, a monument of the sixteenth century. Considered to be the most beautiful building in Faro, and indeed the whole country, it is especially notable for its lovely two-storeyed cloister, which is similar to the Penha Longa cloister at Sintra. The surrounding range of arches is made up of two sets of arches, separated by abutments, topped by highly original gargoyles on the upper floor. The convent was founded by Queen Dona Leonor, King Manuel I's third wife, in the middle of the sixteenth century, and was designed to house the Capuchin Nuns of St Clare. The portico has fine sculpture work dating from 1538 and Corinthian pilasters under the cornice. The coat-of-arms includes a shrimping net.

The convent was abandoned in the nineteenth century and in 1894 it sheltered a collection of art works and archaeological finds formed by Canon Joaquim Maria Pereira Boto. In 1973 it was reconstructed and turned into a valuable archaeological museum, the **Museu Arqueológico e Lapidar Infante D Henrique.** The collection of prehistoric, pre-Roman, Roman, Arab, Visgothic, Gothic, Renaissance, Manueline and Baroque pieces has constantly been enlarged. Here in well laid out display are many treasures of the past. Perhaps the greatest attraction is the Roman mosaic which is nine metres long and three metres wide. In a good state of preservation this lovely mosaic has a portrait of a good looking bearded god of the sea. Also on display are a number of paintings, ceramics, stone coat-of-arms and pieces of fine furniture. Do allow plenty of time to wander around this pleasant museum.

Outside in the bright sunlight it is but a short walk to the **Museu Etnografico Regional** (Regional Ethnographic Museum). Here you can walk amongst rooms laid out as typical Algarve homes with life-like models in local costume. It is a fascinating and cheerful museum.

Many narrow cobbled streets in the old part of Faro, are lined with town houses that have graceful wrought iron balconies. Here the author takes a stroll.

There are two other notable buildings in the Largo da Sé (Cathedral Square). The **Episcopal Palace** dates from the eighteenth century and housed many Portuguese and foreign dignitaries. Its main interest to visitors lies in the glazed tile panels produced by the famous Rato factory in Lisbon, which cover the atrium, the main staircase and rooms on the first floor. The second place of note is the **Diocesan Seminary of Faro,** built on the order of the famous Bishop Dom Francisco Gomes do Avclar. His statue was the work of the sculptor Raul Xavier and has a prime position in the middle of the square opposite the main entrance to the Cathedral.

While in the Old City it is pleasant to walk by what remains of the ancient castle walls and contemplate its violent past history, including the infamous period when England's Duke of Essex sacked and burned the city. Thankfully today's visitors are of a quieter nature and only require some refreshment and souvenirs from the few tourist shops to be found in the Old City.

Arco do Repouso

There are three old gateways to the Cathedral district. Already mentioned is the Arco da Vila. There is also the Porta Nova overlooking the Ria de Faro, which was built to replace an older Porta do Mar and is of little artistic merit. Then there is the **Arco do Repouso.** It was given this name because the gate is made up of two arches, separated by an exposed span and it was here, according to tradition, that King Dom Alfonso III rested and heard mass after the conquest of the city. Nearby is the little chapel **Nossa Senhora do Repouso** (Our Lady of Rest), built at the order of the King in 1709, replacing a niche that already existed. It was rebuilt in 1802 and there is still an image of St George which was used in the Corpus Cristi processions of those days.

Should you decide to leave the Old City by the Arco do Repouso you will have the opportunity to visit the **Church of São Francisco,** a solid edifice which was originally built as a monastery and church for the Third Order of the Franciscan Fathers. Partially destroyed by earthquakes, today it has a single nave and simple facade. However it is worth a visit if you are interested in fine blue and white glazed tiles dating from the eighteenth century. The tiles form a series of panels which depict scenes from the life of St Francis of Assisi. You will also see some paintings referring to the life of the saint: two are signed by the eighteenth-century Italian artist Marcello Leopardi and Liborio Guerini. Annexed to the church is part of the reconstructed monastery, where a small number of Brothers of the Third Order reside; in the same building is a museum collection of valuable wooden images and clerical robes.

Faro city

(Tour Two: about 2½ hours) We start this tour from the pretty gardens, **Jardim de Manuel Bivar,** by the harbour. Car parking in Faro can be a problem. There is some free parking by the Gardens but if it is full, then we suggest that you drive around the little harbour, past the four star Hotel Eva and the large **Harbour Master's Building** (inside is a **Maritime Museum** with model ships and old maps). Look for a car park on the southern side of the pleasure craft basin. You will then have the opportunity to observe, seawards, the Nature Reserve area known as Reserva Natural da Rio Formosa, before you commence your walk.

To the western end of the Gardens you will surely notice a very tall obelisk which is a monument to **Manuel Bivar.** Several streets lead off into the City from this obelisk. But before you enter the main part of the City you may care to visit the **Misercordia Church,** which lies opposite the Garden. This, like all the historical buildings in Faro, has suffered from past earthquakes, fires, and devastation by invading pirates. It is thought that the present beautiful church with its Renaissance portal was ordered to be constructed by Dom Francisco Gomes. The portico is topped by a stone engraved coat of arms and a lovely image of the Virgin Mary. Inside it is lofty, cool, dimly lit and gloriously peaceful. Decorative gilded carved woodwork takes the eye to the high altar.

Next to this church is a building which used to be Faro's hospital, until 1980 when a modern new one was built on the outskirts of the City. Now we are ready to see the shopping and tourist places of Faro. Walking from the Gardens, inland, along **Rua Francisco Gomes** you will be aware that it is a pedestrian walkway so no traffic will spoil your view of the many tiny shops.

Considering that Faro is a major city, it is surprising that there are no superstores. Maybe that adds to its charm, for it is very pleasant to wander the narrow cobbled streets where no two stores are alike, except that a certain number seem to sell a little of everything. Amongst this kaleidoscope of shops you can purchase some high quality goods. Expensive gold and silver filigree jewellery, international fashion wear and well made shoes mingle with the usual souvenirs. The best buys are the attractive hand-painted and glazed tiles *(azulejos),* brass, bronze and copper ware, colourful cotton rugs in all sizes, bedspreads, table cloths and knitwear. The latter are sometimes hand knitted and can be a bargain. Have a look and see how the seams are sewn together to decide if the garment is factory made.

You may well be tempted to purchase some of the delicious looking cakes and pastries, also the marzipan sweets that are formed into the shape of fruits and animals. Along this and a parallel walkway you will find several small cafés and restaurants, patronised by both locals and tourists. The variety of menus include Chinese, Indian and Italian as well as Portuguese. Several restaurants serve fresh fish and sea foods. These are usually priced by weight — so you will be able to see your crayfish or lobster swimming in a tank before you order!

Walking in Faro can become confusing because the maze of narrow streets seems to lead to similar squares *(praças)*. Even the locals have been known to ponder when requested for a direction. However, it is our experience that the residents of Faro are extremely patient and helpful to foreigners, even going out of their way to assist you to your required destination. Nevertheless it is wise to have the assistance of a small leaflet about Faro issued free at the Tourist Office. This contains a reasonable map and marks places like the railway station and bus terminal, post office, hospital, police and market, with places of historical and cultural interest.

The Algarve chimneys

One of the most noticeable features of the Algarve landscape is the *chamine Algarvía,* the highly decorative chimney. Originally they were made from the trunk of a tree, into which an intricate open work pattern was carved. Other chimneys were made of heavy wire with an infill of mortar and sand, but always with a free style pattern. A few of the older chimney tops were formed in ceramics and became exceedingly elaborate and elegant. Some of these master pieces can still be seen today in Faro.

The modern version of the *chamine Algarvía* is usually made in precast cement and painted white. The apertures in the sides are designed to minimise the inflow of wind and rain. Many Algarvíos take a pride in the originality, artistry and design of their unique house top adornment and rarely do you see two chimneys alike. The new villas built in the tourist complexes usually include ornamental chimneys, even if they are just symbolic and there are no fireplaces. It is an intriguing pastime to note the number of different designs observed as you tour the Algarve.

To reach the central market you will leave behind the sleepy old town of narrow cobbled roads and their eighteenth-century houses with sash windows and wrought iron balconies, to make your way up the gentle hill, Rua Dr Justino Cumano, into the modern up-to-date part of Faro. Here the streets are more frantic. The shops sell office equipment, electrical and computer goods, TV, and Hi-Fi, and car sales rooms vie for customers. Your destination for the municipal market is **Largo Doctor Francisco da Sa Carneiro.** This is a large busy square where traffic lights are necessary.

It is good to remember that most shops and offices are open from 0900 to 1300 hrs and 1500 to 1900 hrs, Monday to Friday. A two hour lunch break is normal here. The main **post office** *(corrios)* is downhill in **Rua Doctor João Lucio;** it is always very busy. To the west of the post office, at the beginning of Rua Doctor Justino Cumano, on a small square, is an imposing building, built in 1874 which was once a school for Jesuits. Now it holds the central office of the Algarve branch of the Portuguese Red Cross. Here also is the **Lethes Theatre** (formerly Colegio de Santiago Maior). This Italian-style theatre seats about five hundred people and is closely connected with the theatrical and musical life of Faro.

Continuing down hill via Rua do Lethes, have a look at a fine eighteenth-century house, once one of the residences of the Fialo family. Today it is the School of Hotel and Tourism in the Algarve. Now we turn right into Rua Baptista Lopes and the **Largo de S.Pedro.** This is one of the older parts of the city and once its commercial centre: now it is quieter except for people visiting the **Church of São Pedro.** The church's Renaissance portico has fluted pilasters and the interior has three naves and Doric columns, so characteristic of Faro's churches.

Our next destination is close by, a short walk westwards to the **Largo do Carmo** to see what is perhaps the most unusual sight in Faro — the **Capela do Ossos** (charnel house). First look at the **Nossa Senhora do Monte do Carmo** (church), an imposing building, with two towers rising above the parapet, very much in baroque style. Inside are rich gilded wood carvings, ornate images and valuable paintings on the walls and ceiling. Provided you are not of a too sensitive nature than you may like to visit the aforementioned **Capela do Ossos;** the entrance is by a side door. This nineteenth century vault has 1,200 human skulls and bones used as construction material instead of bricks or stone — an amazing sight but somewhat grisly; we were pleased to get out into the sunshine again. On a more mundane note there is another post office in the **Largo do Carmo.**

Well set off by the ornamental, grey and white cobbled square are the twin baroque towers of the Igreja do Carmo, Faro, which rise above a perfectly balanced facade.

By now you are surely ready to return down one of the many narrow streets that leads back to Jardim Manuel Bivar. Walking around Faro is pleasant if you wish to purchase souvenirs or are prepared to look for its historic buildings. These are still to be seen amongst the more ordinary and rather shabby but newer property. On the eastern outskirts modern Faro has town houses, flats and villas which are neat and tidy but of no real interest to the tourist.

Faro environs

To the south of the city of Faro lies a long spit of land, **Ilha de Faro,** large enough for a line of holiday houses, restaurants, bars and a municipal campsite, **Praia de Faro,** 8 kms from Faro city. To reach there you can take a ferry from the pier at **Porto Nova,** by the old town wall at the eastern edge of Faro. This ferry operates only from June to September. Or you may drive, or take a bus, along the road that leads past the airport and across a single lane causeway bridge with lagoons on either side to sand dunes and a sloping beach.

When it is windy here this is a paradise for wind surfers, but even on calm days the beach shelves quite steeply, so care must be taken when swimming, especially with young children. However, the long stretch of sand makes it fun for sunbathing, beach games and walking. A number of the wooden beach houses are brightly painted and of various shapes and sizes.

Ilha de Barreta, which can only be reached by boat, has a long quiet beach. At the eastern point is the tiny village of Santa Maria and a lighthouse.

TWELVE

Central Algarve: Faro to Lagoa

West from Faro the flat coastline of the Sotavento begins to change. There are still lovely flat sand beaches, but the shore has indentations and coves until, near Albufeira, low cliffs come into view and the more rocky terrain of the Barlovento coast is seen.

Faro to Almancil

Leaving Faro on the fast EN125 main highway westward, 3kms before reaching **Almancil** and to the north of the main road you will see set on a hillside an attractive white church, **São Lourenço.** Some say, quite justifiably, it is one of the most beautiful in the Algarve. This is mainly because the interior is almost wholly covered with blue and white glazed tiles that date from 1730. The work of the artist Policarpo de Oliveira Bernades, these tiles create pictures of the life and martydom of St Lawrence. It is a small church and to come upon so much artistry is almost overwhelming. This feeling is intensified by the sight of the gilt-covered altar and its ornate surround that glistens against the picturesque, blue and white tiles.

After you have admired this country church we suggest that you visit the **Centro Cultural São Lourenço,** which lies almost at the bottom of the hill. The Centro has been founded privately as a centre where young and old may get together to discuss the arts. Housed in a two hundred year old building which has been faithfully restored, it offers a broad spectrum of cultural activities, with exhibitions of Portuguese and international artists, sculptors and artisans. It is also a venue for concerts, classic and jazz, conferences and discussions. It is open from 1000 hrs until sunset. Interested visitors are welcome to just browse amongst the books and handicrafts. Over the last eight years the Centro has become an international cultural community centre. As an added bonus to the artistic decor inside, the terrace and garden are a blaze of colour

Typical of the Algarve in spring this beach at Albufeira is a haven of sunshine.

with numerous exotic plants. Look out for the modern sculpture of João Cutileiro, his distinctive style incorporates the use of various types of natural stone and the movement in his figures is highly original.

Almancil

This is a regional shopping centre, with the EN125 passing through its main thoroughfare. Signposted from Almancil and down on the coast is the prestigious **Quinta do Largo** tourist complex, which is just twenty minutes drive from Faro Airport. Set in two thousand acres of natural pinewoods, and with a seventeen-acre sea water lake used for water sports, this low density development has luxury villas discreetly tucked away. The twenty-seven hole golf course is regularly used for the Portuguese Open Championship. A second, eighteen-hole course is due to open in 1990. Known as the 'ultimate in luxury', the five star Quinta do Largo Hotel is well patronised by the rich and famous international set (see Chapter 4, Hotels). A long sandy beach, riding school and many other sports facilities, together with bars and restaurants all make it an upmarket holiday venue.

A short distance to the west, at **Vale do Lobo,** another luxurious holiday development is well established. It, too, includes a five-star hotel, the Dona Filipa, which belongs to the Trust House Forte Group and has Henry Cotton designed golf courses (see Chapter 8, Golf) that overlook the Atlantic Ocean. Attractive Moorish style villas are set amongst pinewoods. There are good restaurants, pubs, discos, boutiques and banks. In addition there is the Roger Taylor Tennis Centre and many other recreational facilities with four kilometres of golden sands.

On to Albufeira

The next resort in line westwards is **Quarteira** situated along the beach, six kilometres south of the EN125. On the eastern side of town is **Camping Quarteira,** owned by the Orbitor Group. This large site has many A-shape wooden holiday homes that lie in thick pine woods by the beach. The original village of Quarteira has turned into a boom town, with high rise apartment blocks and hotels, stretching along a lengthy promenade. You can use the services of a horse-drawn carriage if you wish to do your sightseeing at a leisurely pace. The fish auctions and market on the seafront make a lively scene. Close by you can make purchases at a large wickerwork market. Some items are made locally and others come from the Portuguese island of Madeira, but quite a lot will have travelled from the Far East.

Stone breakwaters along the beach help to give shelter should it become breezy. Further along are sand dunes with low cliffs behind, a safe place for children to be taken. Right in the heart of this holiday region is the modern tourist complex of **Vilamoura,** 25 kms (16 miles) west of Faro. It is said to be Europe's biggest private luxury development, built on a four thousand acre site. Founded in 1965 by Arthur Cupertino de Miranda, this man-made resort is reputed to be able to house 55,000 people. Within this enormous project are a casino, a yacht marina, first-class hotels, apartments, villas, shopping arcades with restaurants, cafés, bars and discos. Sports facilities include several golf courses. There is even a farm producing fruit, vegetables and fresh milk from cows. It has ultra new designed buildings around the marina that come in all shapes and colours. Equally fascinating are the luxury yachts that are berthed in the little port. If you like the bright life and cosmopolitan atmosphere and all things new and sophisticated, this is the place for you.

In strange contrast to this new development, at the western outskirts of Vilamoura, on the road to Praia da Falesia, are the ancient remains of **Cerro da Vila,** which was first inhabited by the Romans, followed by the Visigoths, and finally by the Moors. We are told these people were here for the fishing, salt and shipping operations. For a small entrance fee you can walk round the old Roman site and view the excavations. Quite easily seen are the elaborate water piping system and some mosaics. A small museum displays artefacts which have been excavated from this site so close to the sea.

Down by the beach, at **Praia da Falasia** are shallow cliffs and a wide beach. Other beaches are **Maria Luisa** and **Olhas de Agua.** The latter has strange rock shapes that rise from the sea but a small fleet of fishing boats still puts out. It is not very good for swimming, but there is a carpark and restaurants and cafés with attractive seaviews.

(Opposite) *This natural stone archway is one of the most visited on the coast. It is at Algar Seco.*

Back on the important main highway: the EN125 has recently been widened to assist the fast flow of traffic. Now the town of **Ferreiras** can be bypassed. But if you want a campsite here, take the road to Ferreiras to the first class **Camping Albufeira** which is part of the Club Albufeira holiday complex. Together with the usual camping facilities (see Chapter 4, Camping), you may use the restaurant, pool-side bars, disco club, supermarket, laundrette, and in the high season there are barbecues and evening entertainment. Tents, caravans, mobile homes and apartments are for hire. There is a regular bus service to Albufeira and the beaches nearby.

Albufeira

Like several other fishing villages along the Algarve Albufeira is one that really exploded in all directions, thanks to the tourist boom of the last ten years. Now it is the largest holiday resort in the Algarve, and in the high season it can be very crowded. Yet the majority of visitors seem to enjoy this 'togetherness' and the cheerful atmosphere of being with fellow holidaymakers. Although it has an international flavour most tourists come from Britain, and English is spoken in bars and restaurants, where menus will be in English.

Historically, Albufeira has held an important position because of its clifftop setting. Occupied by the Romans, Visigoths and the Moors, it was the latter who gave it the name Al Buhera, meaning 'castle of the sea'. Protected by its castle, Albufeira was one of the last fortresses to fall when King Alfonso III expelled the Moors in 1250. In Largo Jacinto d'Ayer, a modern statue honours Vicente de Carvahlo, an Augustine friar who was born in Albufeira. In 1632 Father Carvahlo was burned at the stake in Japan for being a Christian. He was beatified in 1867.

There are three churches of note in Albufeira, the most important one being the **Igreja São Sebastião,** which was built in 1740. Look for the date that is engraved on the arch of the main chapel. It survived the great earthquake of 1755. The largest church is the **Igreja Matriz,** the parish church, which has an ornate ceiling and a triumphant arch over the altar. It also contains many valuable relics of the sixteenth century. The **Igreja Santa Ana** was built to replace a church of the same name destroyed in the great earthquake.

(Opposite) *A panoramic view of Silves with its great cathedral and mighty castle, set above the closely built city. The River Arade lies below the hedgerow.*

Albufeira's narrow streets, some still cobbled, are a real maze but quaint, with small white houses. Buses park on the edge of town; it is very difficult to find car parking space anywhere near the beach, so be prepared to walk.

The main square is attractive with a little park and a lively open air market that spreads out into the side streets. It is especially large on Sundays, when as well as the usual tourist souvenirs it includes live chicks, ducks, rabbits, home-made cheeses, fruit and vegetables from local farms. Some haggling may bring a reduction in prices. Round the square there are several good eating places, some having chairs and tables set outside. This is the place where you can walk around shopping in shorts, even a bikini, without getting too much of a stare. A good selection of shops provide a range of Portuguese made goods, though rather expensive. You need to remember that the shops close between 1330 and 1530 hrs.

The **Tourist Information Office** is on the left hand side of the **Rua 5 de Outubro** very close to the entrance of the tunnel which goes through a high cliff, leading to the short promenade overlooking Albufeira's attractive beach. We can recommend sitting under a sun umbrella on this promenade by the Hotel Sol e Mar, drinking cooled Vinho Verde, while enjoying barbecued sardines and salad. Never does fish taste so good as when it is freshly cooked under the blue skies of the Algarve. On the beach 'the world and his wife' take up every inch of space amongst the weird, sandy rock formations that are so distinctive of this part of the coast. Even in winter time, when the temperature drops, this beach always has its devotees who enjoy walking on the sands.

At the eastern end of Albufeira by the **Largo Cais Herculano,** the fishermen's beach is lined with colourful boats just asking to be photographed. During the early morning you may see these boats returning with their catch. Watch them being hauled in shore. In the olden days oxen were used but now an ancient tractor does the job.

That is the old colourful side of Albufeira, which was created a city in 1986. A more modern picture is found on the outskirts, where much concrete development has led to overcrowding of hotels, apartments and commercial centres. Somehow everywhere seems to be uncompleted and there is little evidence of co-ordination of planning. The area has become vastly over-developed and you have to be prepared for time-share touts.

Around **Monte Choro** are a wide selection of restaurants, cafés and disco bars. Some are British owned, and you are likely to see 'English breakfasts' and 'Traditional English Sunday Roast

Dinners' advertised. You will also find Brazilian, Italian, Indian, Chinese and Spanish cooking amongst the fish and chips, hamburgers, steak houses, sea food and local Portuguese menus. At Tom and Jerry's Bar, by the Bullring at **Areias de S. João** (a suburb of Albufeira) you can take the children for meals and a video show. At night all the family can have a drink and fun with live music. One of the Algarve's top night clubs, Kiss, is open at 2200 until 0400 hrs at Areias de S. João. Albufeira is a cheerful, bright easy-going place, and the 'Brits' seem to love its lively night life.

A long beach: Armação de Pera

Some 44 kms (28 miles) west of Faro Airport and on the coast west of Albufeira and before Alcantarilha, lies **Armação de Pera** which claims to have the largest beach in the whole of the Algarve. When you turn south off the EN125, you will pass two camping parks. On your right is **Camping Canelas,** graded three stars. It is well appointed and much used by Portuguese campers, who leave their caravans on site. On the left a little further towards the sea is **Parque de Campismo de Armação de Pera,** situated about 400m from the

This idyllic beach is Praia de Armação de Pera on an early morning in April. Later in the year it can become crowded.

sea. This is a most favoured place with British campers who especially like to stay during the winter months. They find the camp facilities good, and the special discounts made on long stays make camping in the Algarve just about the most economical in Europe. The fact that this camp has a good supermarket and is within walking distance of the beach is an added attraction. (See p. 47.)

To the east the beach at Armação de Pera is flat golden sand and safe for bathing, then at the western end it changes into a series of rock sheltered coves. On a promontory stands a Romanesque chapel, **Nossa Senhora da Rocha,** Our Lady of the Rocks, dedicated to St Anthony. It is simple inside with a notable painting of a sailing ship wrecked on the rocks and a model of an old Portuguese caravel.

Alongside the lengthy beach, Armação has become a busy tourist centre, with high rise hotels and apartment blocks overlooking the sea. It is a level, pleasant walk along the promenade, but if you wish for something more exciting take a boat excursion to visit a series of caves and grottos: Mesquita, Ruaces and Ponta are well worth visiting. The **Tourist Information Office** is in Avenida Marginal. If you are interested in seeing fish auctions, you must go down to the beach early in the morning. It is an animated scene.

Pottery and wine-tasting: the road to Lagoa

Situated midway between **Alcantarilha** and **Porches,** on the inland side of the road, is the **Artisan's Village.** This is a regular stopping place for coach excursions, popular because in the showrooms visitors are given a short talk about the various liquors on sale and are invited to sample, free of charge, the different wines. ports, brandies and liqueurs. The gift shop has a large selection of Portuguese craft work, leather goods, china, pottery and knitted jackets. It's perhaps not the cheapest place to purchase souvenirs, but very convenient, and the wine tasting makes it a pleasure. However, be restrained if you are driving on!

Continuing westwards along the EN125, by Alcantarilha you find one of the very popular **Water Parks,** this one is called the Big One (tel. 089 32827). It offers *agua e ondras para todos,* water and waves for everyone, with little tots boats, exciting bumper boats, a fantasy area, water chutes and the new wave pool beach. This is the place to spend the whole day, relaxing in the sun, while the younger ones expend their energy safely.

Close by at **Porches** are the well known ceramic pottery shops. People come from afar to buy the colourful assortment of ceramics in all shapes and sizes, including the typical Algarvian chimney pots. For tourists, attractive pottery dishes, candle sticks and bowls make nice presents to take home. But take care, this earthenware cracks easily. More expensive is the Olaria Pottery, whose high quality, hand-painted designs are renowned.

Many visitors to this part of the Algarve make their way to **Carvoeiro,** another quaint little fishing village, often depicted on postcards. The road south off the EN125 is by Lagoa. It becomes rather narrow as it goes downhill to the small shell-shaped beach. Car parking is almost impossible during the high season, if you are unlucky we suggest that you continue about a kilometre eastwards to **Algar Seco** (which means dry gully). It is a pleasant drive past some luxurious villas, all with their own swimming pools and exotic gardens. Should you wish to photograph some of the intriguingly shaped Algarvian chimneys, this is where you will find a splendid selection. Make a stop at a parking space by the Algar Seco rock formations. It is signposted. You can look down over a parapet to see where the red sand cliffs have been eroded by time, wind and sea, creating weird shapes, which now form an interesting picture.

Steep steps (there are over a hundred) lead down towards the sea and concrete platforms, which take you right out over the turquoise waters to watch the waves lash against the rocky caverns below. Everyone goes there to see the amazing double archway of rock, through which is mirrored the sunlit Atlantic Ocean. In the summer season there is a café for refreshments and the toilets are open. Snorkellers like to swim in the clear waters at Algar Seco. You can also visit the grottos on a boat excursion from Carvoeiro.

On your return to the EN125, we suggest that you make a visit to the co-operative Lagoa Winery in Lagoa. You will smell the wine cellars as soon as you step out of your vehicle. The Lagoa wines are the most well known of all Algarve regional drink and have won world fame. The reds have a very clear colour and a delicate taste of fruit. The whites are dry and, when chilled, are refreshing on a hot day. However, the extra degree of alcohol content should be noted.

A drive westwards of eight kilometres from Lagoa, again on the EN125, brings you to the wide estuary of the Rio Arade as it flows out to sea. You must cross the wide span bridge to enter the town of Portimão.

Praia da Vau is a picture postcard beach, where red sand rocks have amazing shapes.

THIRTEEN

Western Algarve: Portimão to Odeceixe

Portimão

Portimão, 65kms (40 miles) from Faro, has always been one of the Algarve's most important centres, because of its strategic position at the mouth of the Rio Adade. A prehistoric settlement, Portimão was occupied by the Carthaginians and Hannibal called it Portus Hannibal. Later the Moors overcame the Visigoths and remained there until they were conquered in 1250 by the Knights of the Order of St James. It was then raised to the status of a town by Dom Alonso III. He named it Vila Nova de Porimao. English, Dutch, Spanish forces and Moorish pirates raided the town. This led to the construction of the fortresses of San João at Ferragudo and Santa Caterina, near Praia da Rocha, on either side of the river, to defend the port.

The earthquakes of 1722 and 1755 did great damage to the town with the sea adding to the disaster. Later the Marquis de Pombal had a hand in the rebuilding and many fine stylish houses are still to be seen near the centre. With the coming of the nineteenth century and the success of the fish canning industry, the prosperity of the town increased. In 1924 Portimão was made a city. Nowadays it is a bustling fishing port and a busy commercial centre.

One of the best views of the City is when you are crossing the bridge over the **Rio Adade,** and can look along its lengthy water front, where large ocean-going fishing boats unload their catch. Modern electronically equipped trawlers *(traineira)* are used in the deep waters of Cabo de São Vicente to fish for tunny and sardines. What a fascinating sight it is to watch small baskets containing slippery, silver sardines being tossed from the hold of the trawler to be caught by a waiting fisherman on the quay.

The fish are immediately coated with coarse salt. Large tunny fish, too, are hoisted out of the boats and it is a hectic scene as the catch is then loaded upon lorries, to go to market for public auction. You can eat some of the rich, tasty sardines at one of the little cafés that line the street by the bridge. Charcoal grilled, they are delicious served with a salad of tomatoes and green peppers. Later in the day you will see the fishermen sitting along the quay, mending their nets.

Try and get to **Portimão** as early as possible in the morning, because, although there is a large car park by the riverside it soon fills, as does parking in the side streets. Perhaps it is more sensible to visit this city by bus, or on one of the many coach excursions starting from the various resorts. The **Tourist Information Office** is at Largo 1st de Dezembro, near the city centre, where you will find a restful park with blue and white tiled benches. The 1st December 1640 is the date when Portugal gained independence from Spain.

Amongst the high apartment blocks Portimão has plenty of shops with some streets for pedestrains only. It is a good place to buy shoes and clothes and the outdoor fish and vegetable market is fun to visit. There is no beach at Portimão. The parish church, **Igreja Matriz,** has three naves with the walls covered by decorative glazed tiles. In the principal chapel is a gold carved panel worked by Manuel Francisco Xavier from Faro. There are two statues; one in wood represents Nossa Senhora Mae das Almas, the other in marble depicts St Peter.

While in the Portimão area, you may like to take a boat trip up the Rio Adade, this follows the route taken by the Romans, Arabs and Crusaders as their boats sailed to Silves, when that city was an important port. There are also boat trips from Portimão to **Praia Tres Irmaos** (the three bears).

It is hoped that by the time you read this Portimão and its environs will have recovered from a massive upheaval caused by the laying of new drains (the outcome of a monetary award from the European Community). This resulted in chaotic road conditions with much delay to traffic.

Praia da Rocha and Alvor

The resort of Praia da Rocha, reached by a turning south off the EN125, owes its origins to the wealthy people from Portimão who built villas there at the beginning of the twentieth century. Some two kilometres from Portimão, at the western side of the Rio Adade,

Praia da Rocha has a splendid coastline situation with a long promenade, running along a shallow clifftop, above a golden beach. This is another seaside resort noted for its curiously shaped sandy rocks and excellent swimming. It really does live up to all the beautiful pictures in travel brochures. However, in recent years, what was a quiet fashionable seaside resort has now, with the building of many high rise hotels and apartment blocks, become a centre of mass international tourism.

One of the first hotels to open its doors, in 1934, was the stately Bella Vista, which has a commanding position on the sea side of the marine road. Formerly a palace, its exterior is in the ornate style of the early twentieth century. Nowadays it is the venue for coach excursion parties, who descend on its gracious interior to take tea and biscuits. Only a few visitors take an interest in its beautiful tiled pictures and period furniture. During the 1930 to 1950 era many British writers and intellectuals stayed in Praia da Rocha and today it is still a popular winter resort with British visitors.

A leisurely way to see the town is to take one of the horse-drawn carriages *(carrinhas)* that are parked along the palm lined promenade. You need to fix the price before the start of your ride.

At the mouth of the Ria Adade the old **Fortaleza de Santa Catarina** has now been turned into an open air café, with tables, chairs and bright umbrellas set on its parade ground. From its commanding position you can enjoy splendid views. There is a tiny chapel, too, with a Gothic doorway.

The wide sandy beach at Praia da Rocha is excellent and safe for children, with sun umbrellas and *pedalos* available. it is worth remembering that the midday and afternoon sun can be very hot, and Praia da Rocha is noted for its high record of sunshine hours. Sailing, windsurfing and waterski are enjoyed here. There are good walks along the cliff top to the west of Praia da Rocha that give marvellous views, especially at **Ponta de João de Arens** (about 4km) where the sea hurls itself on to the rocks and grottos below. Even on a calm day it is a fascinating scene. At low tide you can walk along the sands as far as **Praia de Vau,** where the red sand rocks stand like miniature mountains, dwarfing mere holidaymakers. It really is a lovely situation in winter, when there are fewer visitors about and the average temperature is 57°F (13°C). The coves at **Praia da Batata** and **Tres Irmaos,** where it can be suitable for surfing, are worth a visit.

The nearby town of **Alvor** is 5km west of Portimão and can be reached by a coastal route from Praia da Rocha, or by turning

south off the EN125. Alvor is steadily being built up —
unfortunately in not a very attractive manner — with large high rise
hotels and apartment blocks for tourists (even a casino on the
EN125). Maybe when the developments are completed the town will
look more tidy. Certainly there is a good beach and the old village
is nice. The Carthaginian General Hannibal is said to have founded
the town of Alvor in 436 BC. Later the Moors built a castle here
and here King João II, in bad health, came for a cure. He drank
the water from Caldas Monchique but died here in 1495.

The sixteenth-century parish church has a carved Manueline
portico. The interior has columns of red sand stone, brought from
Silves, and, as in most of the Algarve churches, ornate gilded
woodwork round the altar.

On the outskirts of this sprawling village is a campsite, **Parque
D'Alvor,** overlooking a valley where fig, almond and olive trees
grow (see Page 47). The **Alvor Casino** has an inconspicuous position
on the side road leading to Alvor village.

Back on the EN125 the land is flat and marshy, where the rains
have washed down the soil from the mountains. At **Penina** this level
ground, once a rice field, has been put to good use for here is one
of Europe's top golf hotels, with courses designed by Henry Cotton.
Beautifully set on a low hill the **Hotel Penina Golf** is luxury that is
specially geared to please its golfing clients (see Chapter 4, Hotels).
But even if you are not a golf enthusiast a visit to this famous hotel
is recommended. Delicious lunches are served on the terrace that
overlooks the splendid gardens and swimming pool. The menu in
the gracious Grill Room is superb and the service excellent. Every
night there is dancing to live music. The hotel is owned by the Trust
House Forte Group.

Lagos

The port of Lagos (pronounced Laa-Goosh), 18km (11 miles) from
Portimão, is built beside a deep water harbour and wide bay. It is
steeped in history and still retains an air of being an ancient port,
with its busy fishing boats and narrow cobbled streets lined with
attractive old houses, some having wrought-iron balconies. Going
back in time, the town was named Lacobriga by the Romans and
part of the original Roman walls still stand.

In the eighth century the Moors arrived and were not ousted until
1249, when Dom Paio Peres Coreira gave the town its present

The attractive narrow streets in Lagos have many tourists and plenty of cafés and bars.

name. He also built the fortress walls with their nine towers. Under Portuguese rule Lagos prospered and it became the centre of trade between Portugal and Africa. It was from here that the great armada set off to conquer Ceuta with Prince Henry the Navigator on board. Later the Prince returned to Lagos 'and made it his maritime base, where he organised the building of the famous *caravels,* ships that in due course set sail on the great voyages of discovery to many distant shores. It was from Lagos that Gil Eanes left in 1434 to round Africa's Cape Bojador. There is a nice tale how, prior to his success, no one could get the superstitious sailors to sail in ships that were going round the Cape, because they feared the seas that were always a shining, swirling mass of water. To reassure his men, Gil Eanes ordered his sailors to throw out nets over the raging sea. To their amazement it was discovered that the 'silver' was shoals of sardines, also trying to round the Cape.

Lagos was the birthplace of Saint Goncala de Lagos, the son of a fisherman who entered the Augustinian Order. As a friar he became the composer of holy texts, illuminator of chant books and a remarkable preacher. He is said to have performed miracles for the poor, including the multiplying of fish for the needy. He was made a saint by Pope D Pio VI. There is a statue of him in the **Santa Maria Church.**

Alhough the earthquake of 1755 caused great damage to Lagos, much of the old fortifications remain and have been well renovated. The site of the first **slave market** in Europe is in Lagos, built in 1441. You can see the white arcade with black iron railing round it, at the western corner of Rua da Senhora da Graca, close to the wide **Praça da Republica.** This is a pleasant and wide square with gardens that have a fine exhibition of roses and other cheerful flowers. Notice the mosaic in the design of waves. A fine large statue of Prince Henry seated and looking out to sea, holding a sextant in his hand, is a notable reminder of his important presence here.

Close by in Rua de São Goncalo is the splendid **Igreja Santo António,** a superb example of eighteenth-century Baroque. It is open for viewing every day, except Monday, from 0930 to 1200 hrs and 1400 to 1700 hrs, admission costs 50 escudos. Inside the church your eyes will be dazzled by the gilded wood carvings of warriors, angels and cherubs, all having different features and giving an appearance of movement. No wonder it is also known as the Golden Chapel, even though part of the lower walls are covered with blue and white tiles.

Next door to this church and of equal interest is the **Museu Regional de Lagos,** which contains a wonderful assortment of unusual relics, that range through Roman mosaic, ancient books coins, farm implements, armour and religious vestments to historical pictures. A young woman curator speaks English and is keen to explain about all the exhibits to anyone who will stop and listen. In the somewhat creaking old rooms, you can be wafted back to days of yore.

Out in the bright sunshine you will walk past the **Castle of the Governors** to reach the Rua 25th Abril, with the slave market on your right. Now as you go a little way uphill you will reach a walkway (pedestrians only). On either side are some useful souvenir shops, art galleries, boutiques, restaurants and cafés. To the left and going up a steep hill are the very narrow cobbled streets of the old part of town, where driving is difficult.

Continuing you will come to a division of the way. Take the left hand **Rua Lima Leitao.** Here there is a pavement café where you can enjoy coffee and cakes in continental style. Afterwards a short walk downhill brings you into the **Praça Gil Earnes,** which is the heart of Lagos. A large coloured marble statue stands in the middle of the square, where around the base many visitors congregate. The statue is most unusual. João Cutileiro, has hewn an enormous creation, which in a modern manner depicts King Sebastion, who was killed in battle at Alacacer Quiber at the young age of twenty-four.

Close by are the **Town Hall,** the **Tourist Information Office** and the main **Post Office.** This is a good place to telephone the UK: the post office has private booths and the telephonist will assist you if required. You can also purchase telephone credit cards. On the corner of **Rua das Portas de Portugal** you are likely to find a seller of hot roast chestnuts and stalls selling peanuts and newspapers. The British papers arrive a day late.

Lagos has an undercover market built in 1924. Inside this old building meat and lots of fresh fish are sold on the ground floor; upstairs the flowers, fruit and vegetables make a colourful array and the prices are moderate. Outside the market is a taxi rank. If you walk north along the palm lined seafront for about five minutes you will reach an open space that is the **bus station.** More cafés, bars, restaurants and discos in this part of the town. The pleasant four-star Hotel Lagos is tucked away in a back street behind the bus station. It may be better to park your car on the level before you walk the short distance uphill, although the hotel does have an underground garage.

There are two campsites in the vicinity of Lagos. **Parque de Campismo Trinidade,** is small and uphill at the back of town and near the football stadium. On the way up notice the Stations of the Cross in niches in the walls. **Parque de Campismo Lagos** is a huge green park with a clifftop position, off the Lagos to Sagres road.

Directly east from Lagos is the very long sandy beach of **San Roque** and **Meia Praia,** which can be reached by using the bridge across the river estuary from Lagos. There are plenty of sand dunes and surfing here, but be very careful of currents, especially with young children. Visitors to Lagos who are interested in castles and forts, will enjoy a visit to the **Forte da Porta da Bandeira.** It is on the western seafront. It was built as a defence against pirates and has a drawbridge. The huge gate has the royal coat-of-arms and a crown. You can walk to view the towers, tunnels and entrance ways.

Lagos is a particularly pleasant place to visit or stay. The pace of life here is less frantic than in the central holiday resorts along the coast.

Beaches and fishing villages

Leaving Lagos on the Sagres road, which is still the EN125, as you climb up the hill there is a carpark on the sea side. From here you have some panoramic views of the coastline. You can also see the colourful beaches of **Dona Ana** and **Praia do Camilo.** Steps lead down to the sands where the clear water changes from turquoise to navy blue in the shadow of numerous craggy red sandstone rock. Here some beach bars provide refreshment. Take care, for the sun can be particularly strong in the sheltered coves: sunhats and sunglasses are often required, even on some days in winter. At **Porto de Mos** steps lead down to a secluded beach some 200m long, but it is a long haul back up again. An awe-inspiring view of the coast line and beaches is seen 2km south-west of Lagos, at **Ponte da Piedade** (point of pity). This is a high promontory on which stands a tall white lighthouse and some palm trees. It's the kind of place where you might fancy you can see Prince Henry's caravels, their captains on the poopdeck, setting forth from the safety of Lagos harbour, to brave the wild sea on their voyages of discovery. A long, steep flight of steps leads down to the beach, where you can see grottos and rock bridges.

A little further west along the EN125 is a sign directing you down to the coast at **Praia da Luz** and another wonderful sandy beach. Recently the little village has developed and spread like a mushroom, with villas and apartments; yet the atmosphere is quiet

The newly enlarged harbour at Sagres where there are moorings for private boats as well as the fishing trawlers. Here a mixed catch of swordfish and small sharks is being unloaded.

and restful. It has a number of British residents. On the road leading back to the EN125, the **Valverde Camping Park,** on the left is graded as four stars (see p.48). This is where for the last ten years a number of British 'winter wanderers', with their motor or towed caravans like to spend several months during the winter. Although the good facilities there are reduced in winter, so are the charges.

Further on and south off the EN125 are the quiet beaches of **Praia da Salema, Burgau** and **Boca do Rio.** The first two are fishing villages, but Boca do Rio is isolated and reached by a rough road, where some ruins and archaeological digs are nearby. **Cabanas Velhas** and **Almadena** are other nearly deserted stretches of sand. Further on, the beach of **Figueira** can be reached by car and this is a good place for fishing.

Travelling westwards from Lagos you will be aware of a dramatic change in the scenery. The countryside becomes quite open and only few trees grow, for the strong southwesterly winds blow fiercely here. Some farms manage to grow cereals, and cattle are seen amongst the low hills, One of the joys of this part of the Algarve is the host of wild flowers that, especially in the springtime, spread their colour. Along the hedgerows and amongst the rocky terrain, the grey leafed cistus and the French lavender bloom. Wild rosemary perfumes the air, while along the cliff tops sea pinks cling to the soft soil. Here and there the ubiquitous fig tree is protected by a low stone wall and the tinkle of bells from a herd of goats is heard across the land. Some limestone kilns provide white wash for the Algarvian houses that are traditionally painted twice a year, thus making a background for the pretty green ferns, climbing shrubs and bright potted plants that line the entrance to many country cottages.

Sagres and 'the end of the world'

On the road to **Sagres** and 4km before **Vila do Bispo** is a rural thirteenth-century chapel **Nossa Senhora de Guadalupe,** thought to have been built by the Knights Templar. Tradition has it that Prince Henry prayed here. Notice the ogival portal with an unusual rose window. A few kilometres further on you reach **Raposeira,** a quiet country village where Prince Henry may have lodged. The white parish church makes an attractive picture against the blue sky. On the top of the belfry is a weather vane in the shape of a black cockerel.

Along a border of forest lies **Vila do Bispo.** It is at a junction where the EN125 meets the EN268, which runs north to **Aljezur** and south to **Sagres.** Formerly Vila do Bispo was called Santa Maria do Cabo. The town received its charter in the early sixteenth century and it was donated to the See of Faro, having its own prelate Dom Fernando Coutinho. This gave reason for it to be renamed Bishop's Town, Vila do Bispo. It's a sleepy place; you will find a snack bar by the parish church, which is close to the Lagos to Sagres road. Towards the north of the town, on top of some hills, are some windmills and not very far away is the restaurant O Moinho (the windmill). Now the road takes you into a wild and beautiful, sparse landscape, where you breathe the clean and salty fresh air of the Atlantic Ocean. In olden days this region was called World's End, and even today it is remote

On reaching the village of **Sagres** 26km (16 miles) west of Lagos, you have the choice of either turning right and west out to the peninsular headland or left into the village and port, which is where we will go first. Close to this junction there is access to a beach down a slipway. A few shops, some fishermen's cottages and a very ancient stone cross in a cobbled square are passed, then out on a high headland you can see the **Sagres Pousada** (see Chapter 4, Hotels) and a taller hotel apartment block next to it. Both have fine views overlooking the Cabo São Vicente headland and out to sea.

Before you reach the port you will pass a few eating places. They are usually busy at lunchtime with holidaymakers out on day drives. The road winds quietly down to the sheltered harbour. It comes as quite a surprise to find such a large port, but it is only very recently that proper fish auction sheds and modern mooring facilities have been built. The setting is very picturesque, for the harbour has low cliffs on two sides and both fishing and pleasure boats are moored up here. Should you arrive when the fishing fleet returns with their catch, you may see huge tunny and swordfish, the latter have had their sharp swords removed before being landed. These days fishermen's wives sail as part of the crew and even the children will be allowed on board when the boat is in port. As one would expect, the few restaurants in Sagres have fresh fish on the menu.

Sagres is a way out place, which, when the daily coachload of tourists have departed becomes an isolated outpost of Europe almost surrounded by the Atlantic Ocean, with no more land to the west before America is reached. But before you, too, depart make your way back to the road junction and the mini roundabout and the final road to the west, signed **Cabo São Vicente,** Cape St Vincent.

The Sagres peninsula is a sparse scrubland, where only a few patches of purple heather give colour to the land. However the sheer wilderness with its clear light, steep cliffs and mighty Atlantic creates a natural beauty that makes the journey worthwhile. Against the sky the outline of a tall white lighthouse and an old castle catch the eye. Here history has been made.

Prince Henry the Navigator

At the beginning of the fifteenth century, after the capture of Ceuta in North Africa, Prince Henry was granted some land in the Western Algarve. He returned and set about creating a school of navigation here at Sagres. Around him he collected the most famous astronomers, cartographers and mariners of the day. Away from the distraction of towns these great men observed the skies, drew charts of the oceans and planned the design of new ships. With the Prince's encouragement improvements were made to the sextant and astrolabe. Calculations were made in latitude from the height of stars above the horizon and cartography improved. It was here that the long boat with a shallow draught and a small area of canvas, called the *caravel,* was designed. The large number of masts enabled it to carry square as well as triangular lateen sails which were able to pivot around the mast, so taking advantage of wind from all directions. This, with the use of a stern rudder, made them fast and more easy to handle. From his fortress castle, Prince Henry the Navigator was able to watch his *caravels* sail from Lagos across the ocean and down the coast of Africa.

Today's coach loads of holidaymakers are taken to see Prince Henry's former residence, the **Castle of Sagres,** part of which is now a youth hostel. The walls of the fortress have been carefully renovated and it is impressive to enter the great fort through a deep entrance tunnel. Outside there is plenty of space for parking a car. In a large square on the ground, behind a low chain railing, is what is thought to be a wind compass *(rosa do ventos),* marked out in stones; unfortunately it has become sadly neglected and is being destroyed by weeds. You can climb up on to the ramparts and at one corner of the wall is a stone sundial. The views from here are tremendous. The Portuguese record that much of the original buildings were pillaged and sacked by Sir Francis Drake in 1587 and many of the valuable documents were lost. (Portugal was under Spanish domination and the English were at war with Spain.)

You can now enjoy a breezy walk out beyond the buildings to the edge of the cliffs. This is a good place to throw away your cares to

On the Sacred Promontory of Sagres, Prince Henry's stone compass and sundial now looks sadly neglected, but it is still a wonderful viewpoint.

This small monument was erected to commemorate a visit made by the Brazilian Ambassador to the fortress of Prince Henry the Navigator at the Sagres peninsula.

the wind! The magnificent cliffs are sixty metres high and, below, strong seas dash on the rocky shore. During the afternoon, at 1545 hrs, in a special auditorium, a video film in English tells of the Great Discoveries. Outside is the small **St Catherine's Chapel**, which never seems to be open for tourists, which is a pity.

Before your departure you will have an opportunity to purchase a few souvenirs outside the castle, from local stalls which offer at reasonable prices, packets of figs, almonds, marzipan sweets and honey, also a good selection of woollen jumpers, some of which will have been hand-knitted with the wool from local sheep.

Cape St Vincent

You still have more to see at this far flung corner of the Algarve. The road continues a few kilometres further west so reaching Cape St Vincent, 15km (10 miles) from Vila do Bispo, the most southwesterly point of the continent of Europe. Legend has it that a vessel landed here with the body of Saint Vincent, after he had suffered martyrdom in Valencia, Spain. Since then this headland has been referred to as The Sacred Promontory. Another part of the story is that ravens hovered over the place where the Saint's body rested. Later, when the Saint's relics were removed by sea to Lisbon in 1173, the devoted ravens flew along with the ship. Today in the sacristy of Lisbon Cathedral is an ornamental casket of mother-of-pearl containing the relics of Saint Vincent. In the precincts, attended by the sacristan, is an old raven which is said to have descended from the original ravens. The seal of the City of Lisbon is a sailing ship with a black bird fore and aft.

All that remains now is to visit the famous lighthouse of **Cabo São Vicente,** where you will find plenty of parking space, and probably local women selling hand-made lace and crochet work. In 1846 a lighthouse was constructed and operated with paraffin lamps until 1906, when electricity arrived. Visitors are allowed to enter the lighthouse during the daytime, and climb the seventy-three narrow winding steps to reach the great light of 3,000 Watt bulbs and prisms sending the beam out to sea for a distance of 96 km (60 miles) to where much shipping comes close to round the Cape.

Important naval battles have been fought off Cape St Vincent. In 1693, the French Admiral Tourville defeated an Anglo-Dutch squadron. Later, in 1780 the Spanish fleet was beaten by the English Admiral Rodney; and in 1797 Nelson showed his tactical genius in battle with the Spanish.

The famous lighthouse at Cape St Vincent, which sends its friendly beam sixty miles out to shipping sailing by the most south-westerly point of the Algarve.

On your return journey to Sagres village you may care to stop at **Fortaleze de Beliche,** a ruined chapel and partially restored fortress, which is now a restaurant. Around here the views from the cliffs are spectacular. It is also a popular place with the local fishermen who need to have enormously long rods and lines to reach the sea.

If you are prepared to climb down the cliffs to the beach below at **Tonel,** the underwater fishing and sea beds are worth exploring but you need to be careful as the seas around this coast can be very fierce. Should anyone wish to camp, there is a recently opened site on the northern edge of Sagres village. In the vicinity are new apartment blocks being built. It will be sad if the lovely, wild landscape gets developed for tourism.

The west coast of the Algarve

Returning via the EN268 to Vila do Bispo, we can bypass the town and continue our tour north to see the remaining western coastline of the Algarve. This is a quiet rural ride with very little passing traffic. During April you will notice amongst the trees, alongside the road, some *arbutus* (strawberry trees). The Algarvios use the red berries to make brandy and fruit pies. Both fruit and drink are called *mendronho*. Small farms, heathland and low woodland of umbrella pines make a peaceful landscape.

Down by the coast long stretches of sand at Bordeira, Penedo and Vale Figueira are almost deserted. They can only be reached along narrow roads, sometimes no more than dirt tracks. Just before you reach the village of **Barranco da Vaca,** the EN268 joins with the EN120, which is the main highway from Lagos 24km (15 miles) to the north.

In the small villages you will see old ladies dressed in black with heavy woollen shawls and dark trilby hats, pulled well over their faces, thick black stockings and stout shoes, denoting the hard work done in the fields. The standard of living in the countryside is still very poor compared to that in the southern towns. Bread and fish are their staple diet. So when you see a group of villagers at a small van, it is likely to be the travelling fish man. Not only does he bring fish but all the local gossip, too. The Algarvian peasants are kindly people, courteous and hard working. When not in the fields they will be at home making baskets, chairs, patchwork blankets or lace counterpanes.

Aljezur, 33km (21 miles) from Vila do Bispo, has been inhabited since prehistoric times. Iron, copper and slate have been mined here for centuries. The Arabs were in Aljezur in the tenth century, hence its Moorish name. Eventually the castle was conquered by the Christian, Dom Paio Peres Correia, and King Dinas granted the town a charter in 1280. Owing to its strategic position, on a hill top by a river, it has always had some importance.

Today its castle is in ruins, caused by the earthquake of 1755, although recently some restoration work has been done. Parking in the old town is restricted, but space can be found across the bridge to the north. Here is the **Tourist Information Office,** with a charming lady who will explain, in good English, all you need to know about the area. Behind the office is the local market, which could be useful if you are on a self-catering holiday.

Should you wish to camp and like quiet, remote sites, then we suggest you make for the **Vale da Telha Camping Park** (see p.49). To reach it you must take the EM1003 road just south of Aljezur, and climb up quite a steep hill (possible for caravans), passing through Vales, then on to the EM1004, which is a newly built road in some pine woods, where a new holiday complex is being developed. The large campsite comes as quite a pleasant surprise. It has excellent modern facilities that include a good supermarket. A restaurant is open in the high season. Some enterprising Dutch and German campers have already found this ideal site so suitable for those who enjoy 'wayout beyond anywhere' camping. Close by are the beaches of **Arrifana, Monte Clerigo** and **Amoreira,** all being remote and unspoilt.

If you are not the camping type, maybe it would suit you better to stay at the four star **Hotel Vale de Telha,** which is located 8km from town.

The whole area around Aljezur is rich in game that includes rabbits, partridge, wild boars and wild cats. Birds too, can be heard in the hills, larks, blackbirds, European jays, starlings and ravens. This is a landscape of peace and quiet, with green valleys, fields of melons, sweet potatoes and open spaces with the blue sea beyond. Although the sun shines, it can also be very windy.

From Aljezur to **Odeceixe** is 17km (10 miles), a pleasant drive. But the village of Odeceixe, although old and attractive with cobbled streets, has little to offer except one bar. To reach the beach you must continue downhill and across the bridge over the river estuary, then turn left towards the sea where you may see some white egrets. **Praia de Odeceixe** is a further 4km along a rough road. Be careful if it has been raining.

The river bridge marks the northern boundary of this part of the Algarve, though the EN120 continues on towards Lisbon.

Discovery
"Had the Portuguese not discovered new worlds, twentieth-century man would not be on his way to the Moon."
Colonel Frank Borman, Astronaut.

FOURTEEN

Three inland drives

Inland drive 1
Faro — Milreu — Estoi — São Brás de Alportel — Loulé

Only a few kilometres out of Faro and you find you are in the peace of the countryside. Even driving on the main N2 road (signposted São Brás de Alportel) you will soon be passing cultivated fields, olive groves and orchards full of fruit trees. White-painted farmhouses are bright with red geraniums and the trailing pink and purple bougainvillea, spilling over the old stone walls.

Roman ruins and a derelict palace
In nine kilometres you reach a right-hand turn off (eastwards) to Estoi. If you are driving too fast you will miss it, unless a larger sign has since been erected. But before you get to Estoi you will see on your left the site of the Roman ruins of **Milreu.** Surprisingly there is no proper car park. In 1877 Estacio da Veiga began excavations here and discovered a Roman villa, baths, some attractive mosaic and fragments of columns. Some say the ancient name of this site was Ossonoba (others talk of it as being at Faro). The remains of the round tower standing above ground could be part of a third century Christian church. A number of objects found here, such as the busts of Agripine and Adrian, some pottery and mosaics are now exhibited in the Infante Dom Henrique Archaeological and Lapidary Museum in Faro. Little seems to have been done to preserve these interesting ruins.

Continuing along the same road a further kilometre, you will reach the centre of **Estoi.** Park your car by the large parish church. Your arrival may be observed by a group of black-hatted old men who sit in the shade of an ancient tree. On the opposite side of the road the youths of the village also sit, but on a door step — they, too, will observe your arrival and may give a friendly wave. Now you may take a short walk to the left to where you will see amongst some trees the neglected entrance to the **Palacio do Visconde de Estoi,** the eighteenth-century Palace of Estoi. You can enter the grounds through the gate and walk up the lofty drive, past some tall stable buildings sadly in a bad state of disrepair. Soon you will reach the beginning of a series of formal gardens on several levels. But this is no ordinary garden, being more like the one in Sleeping Beauty, where the time has stood still. Everywhere its past glory cries out for attention. In amongst the weeds are exotic but overgrown plants, and in a small temple there is a cascade over which is a sculpture of the Three Graces. The ceiling and floor are glazed tiles and mosaic. On a high terrace are tall pedestals with busts of various noblemen and marble statues of voluptuous nudes.

The palace is the former residence of the Carvalhal family. The three-storey building is a mixture of baroque, Neoclassic and Romantic styles. Now it is almost empty and in a state of neglect. Hints of its past grandeur are seen in the ornate facade with a high clock tower, elegant windows and delicate wrought-iron balconies.

Part of the neglected ornate gardens and facade of the Palace of Estoi.

The palace has twenty-eight rooms, with the main hall being decorated in the style of Louis XV; the sitting room has ornate plasterwork and paintings of the same period. In the dining room the old furniture is Italian, and the ceiling is painted by José Pereira Jor. It seems very sad that no one is taking care of this once lovely palace.

São Brás, home of the cudgel wielders

The N2 is a fast road and from Estoi junction, it is just seven kilometres to **São Brás de Alportel** (from Faro it is 16kms, 10 miles). This is a spacious town, set between two hills and sheltered from the north wind. It is an attractive place where white-washed houses with red roof tiles and typical Algarve chimneys are set in gardens where almond, olive and carob trees flourish. The name São Brás tells of its Christian origin. The story goes that after the British had sacked Faro in 1596 they advanced on São Brás. The defiant citizens came to meet the foe armed only with clubs and heavy sticks. Such was their ferocity that the invaders retreated and the natives earned the nickname of *Cacha Morreiros* (cudgel wielders).

The white parish church, **Egreja Matriz,** is built in simple classical lines with a tall bell tower. Set in the pavement in front of the church are some interesting tombs. Nearby is a *mirador* which allows good views over the town, and surrounding orchards and green hills. The **Tourist Information Office** is close to the **Largo de Santo Sebastio,** where in a garden there is a monument to the poet Bernardo Ramos who was born here. To reach the **market** from Largo de Santo Sebastio you must drive down Avenida da Liberde, and turn right into Rua Boaventura Passos.

On the outskirts of the town going north and up a steep hill is the government owned **Pousada de São Brás.** It is an outstanding setting, with extensive views which overlook the town and outlying green fields, towards the mountains. This is a peaceful hotel, ideal for a quiet weekend or a honeymoon.

From São Brás de Alportel it is 13km (8 miles) westwards to the market town of **Loulé.** It is a place that is included in a number of the inland coach excursions.

Loulé is an ancient Arab settlement, where you can still find traces of an Islamic past: the covered market is in the Moorish style and many of its artisans are said to be of Arab descent. Conquered by Dom Paio Peres Correia in 1249, Loulé became prosperous. In that time much rock salt was mined and its people were known to excel in making leather, copper and basket wares. During 1291 King

In the smaller country villages, the craft of basketry is performed by both men and women. Their work is usually on sale at the open air markets.

Dinas created the annual medieval Fair of Loulé, which is still held each year. Parts of the strong walls and the castle built in those days still stand: although much was destroyed in the 1755 earthquake, now it has been partially restored. There are several large old churches in Loulé, also museums and art galleries.

A very popular **Sunday Market** attracts crowds of visitors, both locals and tourists. The town police are well geared to cope with the situation, but if you decide to be there on a Sunday, it is best to arrive as early as possible, because by mid morning the narrow streets can be blocked with traffic, even though some are part of a one-way system. Do not let this put you off visiting the town, for in the back streets, leading from the Dom Alfonso II square (in particular, Rua 9 Abril) there are workshops where you can see the craftsmen of Loulé creating lovely copper and brassware, brightly coloured harnesses and filigree jewellery. Loulé is a good place to try some of the regional dishes as there are plenty of bars, cafés and restaurants.

It is here, in February, that the **Carnival Battle of Flowers** is celebrated, with parades, music and dancing in the streets. Easter is the time of the Pilgrimage of Senhora da Piedade, when the Saint's image is taken in procession from its sanctuary, two kilometres outside of the town, to the church, **Igreja de Santo Francisco,** where it stays for two weeks. On the return procession the image is carried by eight men, the *homen do andor,* who run up the hillside to the chapel.

The drive back to Faro is 19kms (12 miles) and takes you again through the delightful Algarve countryside, where early in the morning you are likely to see colourfully harnessed donkey and mule carts, slowly making their way to town with farm and garden produce for the markets. Later in the day, on the return journey, they bring back radios, televisions and videos that are now usurping the folk singing and dancing. Such is progress.

Inland drive 2

Albufeira — Algoz — Silves — Barragem do Arade — São Bartolomeu de Messines — Alte

From Albufeira it is only a short drive to **Ferreiras,** where the EN269, via Algoz, goes to Silves. Those interested in churches should stop in **Algoz,** 12kms (8 miles) from Albufeira, to see the white **Nossa Senhora do Pilar Hermitage** which possesses some seventeenth-century paintings on wood, describing the story of Christ's Passion.

Allow time for driving on this rural road: although traffic is light, some of the route is narrow. The pleasant countryside is dotted with almond, olive and fig trees and the red sandy soil is full of stones. Near to Silves the ground improves and there are groves of oranges, lemons, clementines, grapefruit and pomegranates in the fields.

Silves, once capital of the Algarve

As you approach the fortress town of **Silves,** on the EN124, 62 kms (41 miles) from Faro, you are likely to stop and take a photograph of the great castle set on a hill, with the picturesque town below clustering along the banks of the **Rio Arade** — the same river that flows out to sea at Portimão. Silves has always had a strategic position between mountains and sea. Its origin is very ancient. The Phoenicians were here to trade in ivory and amber, and the Romans came much later. During the seventh century the Moslem invasion began. In those days the Rio Arade was deep and wide and the Arab ships turned Silves into a great trading port. They called it Chelb and it became the capital of the Algarve, with great fortifications and palaces being built, gardens and bazaars. The town thrived as a place of commerce and craftsmanship.

But of course the Arab domination was eventually challenged by the Christians, the Portuguese and the Crusaders attacking the castle. Long battles ensued with the fortress changing hands several times. The final conquest had to wait until 1249 when the Moors were finally ousted. Unfortunately, because of these wars much of the old splendour of the town was lost. To make matters worse the Rio Arade was allowed to silt up, so that the trading ships could no longer reach the town. In 1755, the great earthquake destroyed a large part of old Silves.

The castle, which was restored in 1940, is easily reached on foot or by car, uphill from the main road by the river. You can park in

From the southern walls of Silves Castle are extensive views of orchards and pine-clad hills while seen below, is the yard of a cork factory which is piled with strips of colourful bark.

the cathedral square. The **Sé** (cathedral) was built on the site of a mosque in the thirteenth century, but little of this original Gothic church remains. However, today's edifice is still mighty, with two huge bell towers. Inside you see three naves covered with a wooden ceiling. There are four chapels and numerous tombs, said to be those of Crusaders who helped to capture the town from the Moors in the thirteenth century. On your way out of the cathedral you will be expected to make a contribution towards its upkeep.

Outside it is interesting to look at the **Misericordia church,** whose Manueline doorway is higher than the ground level. Possibly you will be met by young girls who shyly request you to buy some of their rather simple embroidery. Their smiles will make a lovely souvenir picture. Should you require some refreshment or the use of toilets, there is a large busy café near the entrance to the castle.

You enter the **castle** through a gate in the perimeter of the crenellated walls. Inside the castle you will be amazed how spacious it seems, with park-like gardens and colourful flowering trees. A fine larger than life statue of King Dom Sancho I stands armed with a mighty sword as a reminder that you are indeed in a fortress. A walk round the perimeter walls will reward you with panoramic views of the river and town below, and also of the surrounding countryside. At one point you can look over the tops of trees into a cork factory, where piles of the pale bark lie ready to be made into household souvenirs.

Down in the town by the riverside an under cover market is always busy, and outside pavement cafés do a good trade in selling barbecued chicken. Once a month a large outdoor market on the spare land by the river brings in many traders, including gipsies and farmers. It is a lively, noisy scene with plenty of live stock squealing about the place.

The birthplace of a poet
When you leave the town going eastwards on the EN124, the São Bartolomeu de Messine road, do make sure you notice the Portuguese Cross. This small ancient cross is a sixteenth-century symbol of the Christian conquest over the Moors. Carved from a tall piece of limestone, it shows on one side Christ crucified and on the reverse Christ descended from the cross.

Another place to visit lies just off the EN124, north of Silves. It is the **Barragem do Arade** (Arade dam). It makes a nice change from the hot seaside, to come up here for a restful picnic and to look at the huge reservoir surrounded by cool pine trees.

Back on the EN124 you will soon pass by a windmill and reach

São Bartolomeu de Messines 21kms (13 miles) from Albufeira. (The main E01 Albufeira to Lisbon road now bypasses the town, with little traffic through the centre.) The **Igreja Matriz** (parish church) stands out high above the tops of the houses. It is a magnificent sixteenth century building, with a Baroque portal. Inside the three naves are divided by columns and arches. The pulpit is carved marble. The All Souls Chapel is decorated with blue and white tiles. São Bartolomeu de Messines is the birth place of the poet João de Deus, born in the year 1830. His book of poems, Field of Flowers, was written in 1893.

The pretty village of Alte

Still on the EN124, take the turning off leading to **Alte,** said to be one of the prettiest villages in the Algarve. Its name is reputedly derived from *alto,* meaning halt. There is a nice story about a certain noblewoman who, on a long pilgrimage, became exhausted and wished to pray. So she ordered the building of a church there. The present church dates from the sixteenth century. Inside there is only one nave with a pictured vault ceiling. As with most churches in the Algarve, the most impressive features are the blue and white tiled panels depicting winged angels and cherubs on high.

The award-winning village of Alte with its white washed houses and bright flowers makes one reach for a camera. On its eastern edge are the **Fontes de Alte** waterfall and the **Soldos Cave.** When you wish for refreshment, try the restaurant bar, Little Fountain Inn, in the garden of the little fountain.

Should you decide to take a country route back to Albufeira, about 26kms (16 miles), give yourself time to travel at a slow pace since the road is not first class; this will also give you time to enjoy the scenic surroundings.

Inland drive 3
Portimão — Caldas de Monchique — Monchique — Fóia

It would be a pity to be in the Algarve and miss a visit to the mountain regions. One of the most pleasant drives is up to Monchique, on the N266, 24 kms (15 miles) north of Portimão. The Serra de Monchique rises to more than 600m (1968ft) above the surrounding shale ridges and forms a barrier against sea mists which condense on it. The resulting moisture flows down over the rock; this, with the heat, creates a lush vegetation where sugar cane, tropical plants and even bananas can be grown.

An historic spa

Driving out of the busy streets of Portimão, it is a joy to find yourself quickly in the solitude of the open fields. At **Alcalar,** 12kms (8 miles) from Portimão, we see the site of a Megalithic neocropolis, with seven stone pillars. This is the sign of early man in the Algarve. From there on we start to climb on a good road from where we can see the little Rio Boina wending its way down to the sea. How nice it is to see big sturdy trees by the side of the road. Giant eucalyptus, pine and cork trees grow here, such a contrast to the countryside below.

Before reaching Monchique we turn off the main road into a narrow green valley to visit **Caldas de Monchique,** a medieval spa that has been known since Roman and Arab times when there were baths here. Park your car in the small main square and be prepared to go back many years in time. Almost hidden from the outside world is a haven of ancient charm. The Portuguese King João II came here to take the waters and in Edwardian times this was a fashionable place to stay and recuperate from illness.

Hidden away amid the green valley and clear mountain air is Caldas de Monchique, where people go to take the health giving waters.

You, too, may have a taste of the health-giving drink, which is supposed to cure rheumatism, skin ailments and make you feel ten years younger! A modern water bottling plant rather spoils the setting (790 litres of the precious water rises from the ground each day). You are charged a small fee for a glass of it and be prepared for a slightly sulphurous aroma and a bitter taste when you drink it. A number of small tourist shops are situated in an old building and some of the vendors are crafts people who create original jewellery, art work and ceramics of good quality.

Among the Victorian type buildings is an *albergaria* (inn) dated 1691. Surely this must be a romantic place for a honeymoon. Across the road a large bar has a real tavern feeling and one expects a carriage and horses to appear at any moment, full of costumed travellers. Somehow shorts and tee-shirts seem out of place. A strange sight is a British type red telephone box. A little way from Caldas there is a picnic area which has tables set under enormous eucalyptus trees, a lovely spot on a sunny afternoon. Further along the road and opposite a restaurant is a viewpoint which overlooks the Caldas and beyond, down the valley to the coastline.

On the outskirts of Monchique there is a useful petrol filling station and a few souvenir shops. The road is winding and narrow in places, the air fresh and invigorating, in the gardens rhododendrons and roses grow profusely.

Monchique and Fóia

The market town of **Monchique** is noted as a centre of handicrafts. Maybe most of the work is exported down to the coastal resorts, for in town here one sees only a few shops, cafés and restaurants of a simple nature. The parish church is notable for its strange Manueline portal, the stone carving is twisted like rope ending in unusual pinnacles. High above Monchique are the ruins of a 17th century convent. You can walk up to view the outside. Once a month a livestock market is held on a hillside, near the town.

To reach Fóia you will need to drive up a very narrow, steep, cobbled road leading off the town's central square. Fortunately it is a one-way system, and on your return downhill you will exit on the southern outskirts of town. It is eight kilometres (5 miles) from Monchique to **Mount Fóia,** which at an altitude of 902m (2959 ft) is the highest point in the Algarve.

The first part of the winding drive takes you past mimosa, eucalyptus and pine trees. Then the view opens and you leave the vegetation below. Hopefully you have chosen a clear day so that you can enjoy the very extensive views of the surrounding bare ridges which give you an 'on top of the world' feeling. A radio/television mast rather spoils the vista, but it is nice to see that some heather survives at this high altitude. On fine days your panorama allows you to see as far as the Sagres peninsula, Lagos Bay and the coastline around Portimão. An obelisk here marks the highest point in the Algarve. Souvenir vendors appear with the tourist coaches. Should it be misty or raining on your descent to the coast be careful of the twisting roads and the coaches, who expect you to give way for them. As you drop down the lush green mountain, it is hoped that you will feel refreshed, even if the 'ten years younger' is only a myth.

Village vignette

When you leave the Algarve coast behind, you notice a change in the landscape. As you travel further north the fertile land gives way to a more rugged countryside. Life, too, becomes harder for the quiet Algarvian peasants who have to till the harsh land with a mattock *(enxada)* to remove stone after stone before they can reach the soil. These stones are then used to make low walls which act as wind breaks. Few of these villagers are yet able to afford the modern machinery that would make life easier.

In the upper country areas of the Algarve the washing is still done down by the bridge where the water flows steadily, and the clothes are beaten clean on the stones. Later the laundry is laid out on nearby walls or bushes to dry. Although most rural communities now have running water, many like to collect it fresh from a natural spring.

Farmers cultivate cork and olive trees, with a few figs, walnuts and chestnuts. The umbrella pine *(o pinheiro manso)* grows long and strong, with its squat cones ripening in February and March. These yield hard shelled pine nuts *(pinhaos)* whose kernels have a delicate flavour. Working in pairs, husband and wife shake and beat down the cones, which then have to be pounded between two stones until the kernelss are free. A long day's work may yield just twelve to fifteen kilos of nuts. Then these pine nuts are used to make sweets similar to the more familiar sugared almonds. They are popular at Easter time, when they are offered as gifts.

During the long winter evenings, older women are at work on a variety of woven or sewn bedcovers and rugs, made from odd scraps of material. Often these are in a patchwork design. Thick woollen shawls, with long fringes, are knitted from virgin wool dyed black. They are almost standard wear for the peasant women and sell well at the local market or fairs, but rarely do they reach the shops. The quiet creativeness of these women, and the patience of their toil, is these days only to be found in the uplands of the Algarve.

Finale

For centuries travellers have found pleasure in visiting the Algarve with its bright sunshine. Today its relatively pollution-free beaches are an added attraction. History tells of the brave Algarvians who went forth from this gentle land. Today, these quiet, polite people give a courteous welcome to their many visitors. We hope that, as well as enjoying the modern pleasures of hotels, casinos and nightlife, you will spend time exploring the cheerful markets and drive amongst the orchards and farmland. Go down the narrow streets of old towns and walk in the fragrant air of the pine forests.

Life still remains its unhurried way and, personally, we think the stable character of the Algarvians has real charm. We trust that you will enjoy being here.

> Gentle Algarve, where sand and sea meet
> once brave caravels sailed on the tide,
> now new age discoverers to your shores arrive.

Portuguese/English Vocabulary

Useful words

bom dia	good morning	*quanto custa?*	how much?
boa tarde	good evening	*bom*	good
boa noite	good night	*mau*	bad
até à vista	good bye	*ghrande*	large
sim	yes	*pequeno*	small
nao	no	*selo*	stamp
por favor	please	*chave*	key
obrigado	thank you		

Services

a padeiria	bakery	*a lavandaria*	laundry
o banco	bank	*a biblioteca*	library
o barbeiro	hairdresser	*o mercado*	market
a livraria	bookshop	*o oculista*	optician
o talho	butcher	*o posta da*	
a pastelaria	cake shop	*polícia*	police station
a farmácia	chemist	*a estação de*	
lavanderia a		*correios*	post office
seco	dry cleaner	*a sapataria*	shoeshop
a peixaria	fishmonger	*a papelaria*	stationer
o lugar de frutas		*o supermercado*	supermarket
e legumes	greengrocer	*agência de*	
a mercearia	grocery	*viagens*	travel agent
o hospital	hospital		

Public signs and notices

esquerdo	left	*estacionamento*	parking
direito	right	*estacionamento*	
aberto	open	*probido*	no parking
fechado	closed	*paragem*	bus stop
em cima	up	*pasagem*	
em baixo	down	*probido*	no entry
livre	free (vacant)	*perigo*	danger
ocupado	occupied	*polícia*	police
pare	stop	*senhoras*	ladies
cruzamento	cross roads	*homens*	gentlemen

Food

alho	garlic	*flãn*	caramel mould
ananaz	pineapple	*frango*	chicken
arroz	rice	*gambas*	prawns
assado	roast	*guisado*	stew
atum	tunny fish	*lagostin*	lobster
azeitonas	olives	*limão*	lemon
bacalhau	cod fish	*linguado*	sole
banana	banana	*lulas*	squid
bife	beef steak	*mariscos*	shell fish
bolo	cake	*ova*	egg
biscoitas	biscuits	*porco*	pork
borrego	lamb	*presunto*	ham
cebola	onion	*queijo*	cheese
chourico	spiced sausage	*salsichão*	salami
coelho	rabbit	*sopa*	soup
costeletas	chops	*torrado*	toast
ervilhas	peas	*uvas*	grapes

Drink

água	water	*cha*	tea
cerveja	beer	*vinho tinto*	red wine
café	coffee	*vinho branco*	white wine
leite	milk		

Restaurant

un copa	glass	*batatas*	potatoes
talheres	cutlery	*peixas*	fish
paõ	bread	*carne*	meat
manteiga	butter	*legumes*	vegetables
sal	salt	*frutas*	fruit
pimenta	pepper	*sopa*	soup
mostarda	mustard	*açúcar*	sugar
ova	egg	*um gelado*	ice cream

Days of the week
(note that capitals are not used in Portuguese)

domingo	Sunday	*quinta-feira*	Thursday
sequnda-feira	Monday	*sexta-feira*	Friday
terça-feira	Tuesday	*sabado*	Saturday
quarta-feira	Wednesday		

Months

Janeiro	January	*Julho*	July
Fevereiro	February	*Agosto*	August
Março	March	*Septembro*	September
Abril	April	*Outubro*	October
Maio	May	*Novembro*	November
Junho	June	*Dezembro*	December

Numbers

0	*zero*	26	*vinte e seis*
1	*um, uma*	27	*vinte e sete*
2	*dois, duas*	28	*vinte e oito*
3	*três*	29	*vinte e nove*
4	*quatro*	30	*trinta*
5	*cinco*	40	*quarenta*
6	*seis*	50	*cinquenta*
7	*sete*	60	*sessenta*
8	*oito*	70	*setenta*
9	*nove*	80	*oitenta*
10	*dez*	90	*noventa*
11	*onze*	100	*cem*/cento*
12	*doze*	200	*dezentos*
13	*treze*	300	*trezentos*
14	*catorze*	400	*quatrocentos*
15	*quinze*	500	*quinhentos*
16	*dezasseis*	600	*seiscentos*
17	*dezassette*	700	*setecentos*
18	*dezoite*	800	*oitocentos*
19	*dezanove*	900	*novecentos*
20	*vinte*	1000	*mil*
21	*vinte a um*	1100	*mil e cem*
22	*vinte e dois*	2000	*dois mil*
23	*vinte e três*	5000	*cinco mil*
24	*vinte e quatro*	100,000	*cem mil*
25	*vinte e cinco*	1,000,000	*um milhão*

(*cem is used before nouns and adjectives)

Useful phrases

Do you speak English?   *Fala inglês?*
Could you speak more slowly, please?   *Pode falar mais devagar, por favor?*
Please write it down.   *Escreva, por favor.*
I do not understand.   *Nao compreendo.*
Can you help me?   *Pode ajudar-me?*
I would like.   *Queria.*
I am lost.   *Perdi-me.*
Where is a restaurant?   *Onde é o restaurant?*
Is there a bus?   *Ha um autocarro?*
Where can I get a taxi?   *Onde posso apanhar um taxi?*
What is the fare to.....?   *Qual e preco do percurso para.....?*
Take me to.....   *Leve-me*
I am in a hurry   *Estou com pressa*
What is the price?   *Qual é o preço?*
I am hungry/thirsty   *Tenho fome/sede*
My name is.....   *Chamo-me.....*
What is your name?   *Como se chama?*
How are you?   *Como está?*
How much is this?   *Quanto custa isto?*
I need a doctor   *Preciso de um médico*
I have toothache   *Tenho dor de dentes*
I have lost my passport   *Perdi o passaporte*

Appendix B
Wind Force: The Beaufort Scale*

B'fort No.	Wind Descrip.	Effect on land	Effect on sea	Wind Speed knots	mph	kph	Wave height (m)†
0	Calm	Smoke rises vertically	Sea like a mirror	less than 1			-
1	Light air	Direction shown by smoke but not by wind vane	Ripples with the appearance of scales; no foam crests	1-3	1-3	1-2	-
2	Light breeze	Wind felt on face; leaves rustle; wind vanes move	Small wavelets; crests do not break	4-6	4-7	6-11	0.15-0.30
3	Gentle breeze	Leaves and twigs in motion wind extends light flag	Large wavelets; crests begin to break; scattered white horses	7-10	8-12	13-19	0.60-1.00
4	Moderate breeze	Small branches move; dust and loose paper raised	Small waves, becoming longer; fairly frequent white horses	11-16	13-18	21-29	1.00-1.50
5	Fresh breeze	Small trees in leaf begin to sway	Moderate waves; many white horses; chance of some spray	17-21	19-24	30-38	1.80-2.50
6	Strong breeze	Large branches in motion; telegraph wires whistle	Large waves begin to form; white crests extensive; some spray	22-27	25-31	40-50	3.00-4.00

Force	Name	Land description	Sea description				
7	Near gale	Whole trees in motion; difficult to walk against wind	Sea heaps up; white foam from breaking waves begins to be blown in streaks	28-33	32-38	51-61	4.00-6.00
8	Gale	Twigs break off trees; progress impeded	Moderately high waves; foam blown in well-marked streaks	34-40	39-46	63-74	5.50-7.50
9	Strong gale	Chimney pots and slates blown off	High waves; dense streaks of foam; wave crests begin to roll over; heavy spray	41-47	47-54	75-86	7.00-9.75
10	Storm	Trees uprooted; considerable structural damage	Very high waves, overhanging crests; dense white foam streaks; sea takes on white appearance; visibility affected	48-56	56-63	88-100	9.00-12.50
11	Violent storm	Widespread damage, seldom experienced in England	Exceptionally high waves; dense patches of foam; wave crests blown into froth; visibility affected	57-65	64-75	101-110	11.30-16.00
12	Hurricane	Winds of this force encountered only in Tropics	Air filled with foam & spray; visibility seriously affected	65+	75+	120+	13.70+

* Introduced in 1805 by Sir Francis Beaufort (1774-1857) hydrographer to the Navy
† First figure indicates average height of waves; second figure indicates maximum height.

APPENDIX C: USEFUL CONVERSION TABLES

Distance/Height

feet	ft or m	metres
3.281	1	0.305
6.562	2	0.610
9.843	3	0.914
13.123	4	1.219
16.404	5	1.524
19.685	6	8.829
22.966	7	2.134
26.247	8	2.438
29.528	9	2.743
32.808	10	3.048
65.617	20	8.096
82.081	25	7.620
164.05	50	15.25
328.1	100	30.5
3281.	1000	305.

Weight

pounds	kg or lb	kilograms
2.205	1	0.454
4.409	2	0.907
8.819	4	1.814
13.228	6	2.722
17.637	8	3.629
22.046	10	4.536
44.093	20	9.072
55.116	25	11.340
110.231	50	22.680
220.462	100	45.359

Distance

miles	km or mls	kilometres
0.621	1	1.609
1.243	2	3.219
1.864	3	4.828
2.486	4	6.437
3.107	5	8.047
3.728	6	9.656
4.350	7	11.265
4.971	8	12.875
5.592	9	14.484
6.214	10	16.093
12.428	20	32.186
15.534	25	40.234
31.069	50	80.467
62.13	100	160.93
621.3	1000	1609.3

Dress sizes

Size	bust/hip inches	bust/hip centimetres
8	30/32	76/81
10	32/34	81/86
12	34/36	86/91
14	36/38	91/97
16	38/40	97/102
18	40/42	102/107
20	42/44	107/112
22	44/46	112/117
24	46/48	117/122

Tyre pressure

lb per sq in	kg per sq cm
14	0.984
16	1.125
18	1.266
20	1.406
22	1.547
24	1.687
26	1.828
28	1.969
30	2.109
40	2.812

Temperature

centigrade	fahrenheit
0	32
5	41
10	50
20	68
30	86
40	104
50	122
60	140
70	158
80	176
90	194
100	212

Oven temperatures

Electric	Gas mark	Centigrade
225	¼	110
250	½	130
275	1	140
300	2	150
325	3	170
350	4	180
375	5	190
400	6	200
425	7	220
450	8	230

Your weight in kilos

stones

kilograms

Liquids

gallons	**gal or l**	litres
0.220	1	4.546
0.440	2	9.092
0.880	4	18.184
1.320	6	27.276
1.760	8	36.368
2.200	10	45.460
4.400	20	90.919
5.500	25	113.649
10.999	50	227.298
21.998	100	454.596

Some handy equivalents for self caterers

1 oz	25 g	1 fluid ounce	25 ml
4 oz	125 g	¼ pt. (1 gill)	142 ml
8 oz	250 g	½ pt.	284 ml
1 lb	500 g	¾ pt.	426 ml
2.2 lb	1 kilo	1 pt.	568 ml
		1¾ pints	1 litre

Bibliography

Frank Cook *Algarve,* (1971) Faro, Algarve: Publicaoes Frank Cook.

Henry Myhill *Portugal* (1972) London: Faber and Faber. ISBN 0 571 096409

Portugal, Madeira (1972) Michelin Tyre Co. Green Guide. ISBN 206 121 500 9.

Charles E. Wuepel *The Algarve* (1974) David and Charles ISBN 07153 60388.

Kathryn Braund and Deyanne Farrell Millar *Portuguese Water Dog* (1986) New York: Howell Book House. ISBN 087605 262 6.

Mary McMutrie *Wild Flowers of the Algarve* (1986) Vila Real de Santo António, Algarve: Empresa Litografica do Sul.

Maria Beatriz Condess *Algarve Guide to Walks* Faro, Algarve: Regional Tourist Office.

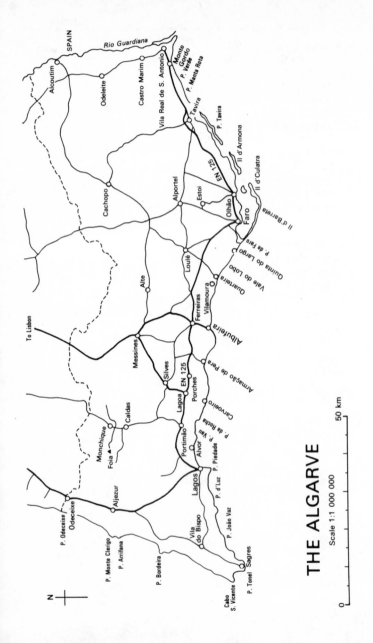

THE ALGARVE

Scale 1:1 000 000

0   50 km